The Urban Farmer's Handbook

By Paul Peacock

Published by The Good Life Press Ltd. 2008
Copyright © Paul Peacock

ISBN 978 1 90487 127 9
A catalogue record for this book is available from the British Library

The Good Life Press Ltd.,
PO Box 536, Preston, PR2 9ZY

www.goodlifepress.co.uk
www.homefarmer.co.uk
www.precycle-it.co.uk

Set by The Good Life Press Ltd.
Drawings by Rebecca Peacock, additional drawings by Paul Melnyczuk

The Urban Farmer's Handbook

By Paul Peacock

Contents

Introduction Part 1

What Makes an Urban Farmer?

There are already a lot of obstacles to being a farmer in an urban situation, but equally there are pressing matters. Soon, sooner than we all think, and sooner than the pundits used to buying their stores and provisions from the supermarket will admit, we are going to have to be responsible for our own food.

The expansion of the nation's farming industry is never going to produce enough food for the growing population of the country and once again we will be encouraged to "dig for victory." So what makes an Urban Farm?

The answer is simple; a farm is a space set aside for the production of food. An Urban Farmer is simply the producer of his own food.

When I was a child the USSR wanted to send missiles to the small Caribbean Island of Cuba. Quite naturally the Americans didn't like it and we were all scared to death of a world conflagration. The Russians backed down and we all forgot about Cuba. Over the years they sold sugar to Russia at such an inflated price that Cuba became a very rich nation. When Communism floundered, Cuba's money ran out and they were faced with disaster. No food, no power, nothing. So they came up with a novel solution – every spare plot of land in the cities and villages was turned over to food production, a kind of collective allotment where people who lived in apartments could grow as much of their own food as possible. Their model was the British Dig for Victory movement, with a touch of Marxism thrown in for good measure.

Cuba was lucky because their amassed wealth kept them going for a year or two until their rushed system kicked in and by then they were already used to low rations. I don't think we are in for the same easy ride.

How much land you need for self-sufficiency depends on what you want to eat. Even a garden can produce a prodigious amount of food, if you want to be a vegetarian. An allotment sized space can produce all the vegetables you will ever need. A second space will provide all the fruit you will ever need and enough space to grow sunflowers and sweetcorn in sufficient quantities to keep a small flock of hens for meat and eggs.

Every family, in my opinion, should keep bees. They gather a crop from all over the countryside and from everyone's back garden, and this dramatically improves your own effective crop. A hive full of honey, as much as 50 kilos of honey, is a remarkable thing and is enough for cooking, sweetening, preserving and, of course, brewing!

I would consider that a beehive is more important to the running of the urban farm than even chickens because without them we have no opportunity of pollinating our crops.

Of course, in order to maintain fertility animals are important in producing manure. But you have to be sure about where the nutrition comes from. If you grow your own food for chickens and your own vegetables and you compost only the things that come from your garden farm, you are going to find the fertility doesn't keep up with the production. Regardless of the nature of your rotations, the small size of urban farms renders them of little use. Crop rotation to maintain fertility works on a field scale, not on a garden scale. Therefore YOU MUST BRING IN FERTILITY from outside the garden, either in the form of chemicals, rock dust or probably more importantly, from farmyard manure.

Secure a supply of muck that came from animals not fed on your own crops and compost it. This will be the heart of your fertility. If you had five acres of grassland from which you made hay to feed a cow for the year and used the manure to feed your garden, this would be enough to maintain its fertility. The fields would almost look after themselves because their large area would accumulate enough nitrates from the atmosphere to cope with the hay crop.

Gardening with animals is, you might think, a far cry from Urban Farming, but why should it be? On the whole this book will concentrate on the ordinary semi-detached garden and associated house. There are so many millions desperate to get extra land, but might never manage it. There are reasons, however, to include the keeping of cattle and pigs in this scheme of things. For example, I live in the inner-city. I do not have an allotment and neither do I have much land other than a ten metre square patch. But in this I can grow most of my own potatoes, salads, root crops, some of my fruit and both chickens and bees. I am by no means self-sufficient, but near me is an old farm with a field which I could rent along with a number of other families to keep a cow, and maybe some pigs and some geese.

Everyone's garden can be a place for making food and, when you look around, there are plenty of places for growing more that are probably unused. When I was a student I did some research on the pollution from cars. Tetraethyl lead was an additive that deposited the heavy metal on the pavement. It was quite plain that the land up to 100 metres from any main road was heavily contaminated with the material, but it fell off sharply after that – no wonder really as lead is heavy after all! Anyway, today there is no additive in petrol that pollutes in the same way, so there is now no reason for not lining your front garden, the fence or wall and even an amount of the pavement with pots containing crops. This kind of planting can effectively double your area for food production if you have a small garden. If you include hanging baskets and terraced walls of pots too, you will be amazed how much you can cram in. Gain the space of a car too by parking on the street and planting on the drive. You can draw in the garage roof and any other area you can find, so long as it is safe and convenient to do so.

Around the neighbourhood there are also plenty of great places to grow crops, but keep to pots because you do not necessarily know the state of the soil. Heavy metal contamination is unseen yet insidious and poisons such as mercury, arsenic, thallium, chromium and many others reside in soils left behind by industrial processes. Plants growing on these soils will have various levels of contamination from zero to significant. You are always best to make sure the food you grow is separated from old soil in any urban situation. That goes for your garden too! Just because you may live in a new house it doesn't mean to say your soil is either new or safe, so make sure you find out about the history of your soil.

You can get a good idea from old OS maps of what has been on your plot before you and if you are at all unsure you will need to play safe. The immediate answer to this is to grow in raised beds with new soil and new compost. You can line the beds with pieces of slate; a trip to Llanberis in North Wales will do the trick, or any suitable material, then grow on top of this. This also applies if you are keeping livestock on any polluted or contaminated land.

Air Pollution

There are limits to what factories can pump into the air, but that doesn't mean they don't! Near me is a factory that makes foam materials for furnishings and the smell of aromatic chemicals when they are making a batch is truly awful. I found it on a website that described it as one of the major polluters in the country, but when I asked them about it they simply refused to answer my emails.

There are few things we can do about the pollution around us in the city. Some of it is old, some new, but I believe we should fight to make the world a cleaner place. One thing I do know is that I will not use the eggs produced for a week after the foam company have been making up a batch just in case!

Water Pollution

If you can, make sure you only water with rain collected from rooftops and sheds. If you have a well or a spring supply, have it tested – it has become mandatory for regular tests anyway. In an urban situation you cannot trust ground water to be clear of pollutants. The river Irk that runs from Rochdale to Manchester is heavily polluted still, even though most of the industry that once spilled its guts into it has now gone. Actually, for the first time in many a year you can now see young trout in it – but I wouldn't wish to eat them just yet!

Runoff from roads is highly poisonous, especially following a period of dry weather. Chemicals in the rubber from vehicle tyres are washed off the carriageway into the system and this feeds the rivers with a great deal of pollution.

Guerrilla Gardening

With all these matters in mind it is best, if you are going to grow crops out in the wider world, to be absolutely sure of the inputs into that system. Wherever possible, grow plants in pots and leave them in secure places. A friend who was the last tenant in a high rise block of flats put plant pots on the balconies of all his empty neighbours.

Car Parks and factory spaces are ideal places for growing in pots – you can make yourself a huge array of imaginative places to grow foods that are in themselves separate from your own land, but people would hardly know they are there.

City Centre Growing

We have already mentioned the need to grow food in cities. If you work in the city centre, ask your employer if you can have a small corner of anywhere suitable to grow food. You can tend to it in your lunchtime. If you go up in a helicopter you will see a large green area that, from ground level, looks just like an urban wasteland. So get yourself some containers and grow some food there! I always feel that sunflowers are best for urban spaces because they look good and non-gardeners might not think you quite so odd. No one really complains about seeing beautiful plants.

The thing about Urban Farming is that it is imaginative. There are organised city farm movements and these are great places to visit and learn. There are people who live in mobile homes who grow food in all kinds of places so they can harvest them as they travel around the country. There are narrow boat owners who have plant pots on their roofs filled with herbs. There are lots of possibilities out there, but only one true imperative – must grow food, in cities, on allotments, in gardens, in streets. That's the thing about new urban farming, it is creative.

The Urban Farmer

Introduction Part 2
The Economics, Ecology and the F Word

It is amazing how beautiful the countryside is. We have just completed a journey the length of the country and it is wonderful to see fields and hedges, returning wildlife, mountains, river and sea. Then I noticed something that was at first interesting and then, as the trend repeated itself, quite alarming. It sounds petty, but you can tell you are approaching a town or a city by the number of horses you see in the fields. Now I have nothing against horses, or even people who ride them. I myself have never managed to find a horse stupid enough to carry my weight but that doesn't make me peevish against those that have.

What this little trend shows is the change in the world over a generation or two. At one time, if you travelled between two great cities, say Manchester and Liverpool, the land between was busily used growing all the vegetables those cities needed. When I was at school we used to call it the hinterland. The land between the said two cities used to be filled with growing potatoes, cabbages, carrots, cauliflowers, swedes and the like. There used to be huge greenhouses, and I mean huge, growing tomatoes and lettuces.

But it's not only 'Up North' where this took place. The land now occupied by Heathrow Airport used to be the market garden for London. Every city and town had its own special place to grow crops for its inhabitants and generally they were fresh, wholesome and good. The nation of shopkeepers were fed by a myriad of small growers who lived outside the town, but no more than a couple of hours horse journey away. Have you noticed that the market towns of Southern England are 30 miles apart from each other in a sort of a grid? A small farmer was never more than 15 miles from his nearest market, maybe 2.5 hours with his pony and maybe 4 hours on foot.

This system worked for the better part of 7 centuries but started to die away because of trade and fertility. In the 1850s the smell of the polluted Thames forced the government to build sewers to wash away the night soil (pooh to you and me) rather than have it floating down the river. This improved the health of Londoners no end. But not all of the human waste went into the river. Some of it was composted and carted to Middlesex as fertiliser for the market gardens that fed the capital. Other cities had similar schemes. Night soil was collected and taken to what is now the City of Manchester Stadium to make what they called Manchester Compost. This was carted to the Ormskirk region for the same purpose.

As more people were connected to the flush sewers, less fertility reached the land, and market gardening became harder.

Two other trends also helped to kill the market gardens. The first was the realisation that you could equate food with money. You put seed in the ground that cost less than a hundredth of a farthing and sold the lettuce for thrupence. Multiply this by a field and you get a lot of money. Multiply this by a lot of farms and you have it made. From the times of the enclosures, British farms have been amalgamated over and over. In a one acre field you can get maybe a tonne and a half of wheat, but in a two acre field you can get four tonnes. A ten acre field will give you 60 tonnes, and they are easier to work. It wasn't the farming, nor even the crop, but the money it represented that became important. And it certainly wasn't the people that mattered either. When cheap corn was available from Europe the government protected their wealthy members by imposing a tax on it until it matched the price landowners wanted for their home grown corn. In early Victorian England children starved even though there was plenty of corn to make bread. It was just ordinary people that couldn't afford to buy it.

Then trade itself combined to set the market garden into redundancy. This is a more modern phenomenon. British farming was in the doldrums before the Second World War, and when we were under siege by Germany there was not much to be had. A huge effort on the land was backed up by a flotilla of ships from America and we never looked back.

Why buy a tomato from the UK which comes in a glut but is unavailable for the rest of the year when you can buy them from all around the world at any time and fly them into the UK? Consequently our market gardens are now no longer just outside our cities but are found everywhere on the planet. Tomatoes come from Spain, Chile, Kenya, the Far East, and so do most of the other things we eat. The fields outside our cities have become industrial estates, housing estates, fun farms where people flock to see animals, or have become motorway verges. London's market gardens became Heathrow airport, and in a way it still feeds the capital today, but now via the whole world.

But times are changing. This whole system came about because the provision of food is dominated by money. But what happens when the value of money reduces? What happens when we can no longer make enough money to buy our food from the far flung corners of the world? Or more to the point, when the big powers on the planet out compete us in buying power for the limited food the planet grows? Since we no longer are able to feed ourselves, what will happen when the shortfall isn't met from elsewhere?

This is all well and good, painting a black picture about the future of our food supplies, but there are other considerations. In a world where the oil economy is facing its final days, the transportation of food around the world in aeroplanes and container ships cannot have a sustainable future. Transporting tomatoes or Kiwi fruits from New Zealand pumps far more CO_2 into the atmosphere than the weight of the product and costs so much more energy than the product contains. How can that be sensible?

The Laws of Human Ecology

A number of workers in the USA did some fundamental thinking from the 1930s onwards, a long time before current Eco-Movements. They predicted modern problems and came up with the idea of misery. Misery was all those factors that combine to reduce the human population; poverty, war, starvation and disease – literally misery. That being the case, the following statements make up the basis of human ecological thinking:

Boulding's Three Theorems

Kenneth Boulding was the founder of the evolutionary economics movement. In his "Economic Development as an Evolutionary System," Boulding suggests a parallel between economic development and biological evolution. (Yes, there is a point to this!)

His first theorem of human ecology was called "The Dismal Theorem"

"If the only ultimate check on the growth of population is misery, then the population will grow until it is miserable enough to stop its growth."

This is followed by his second theorem: "The Utterly Dismal Theorem"

"Any technical improvement can only relieve misery for a while, for so long as misery is the only check on population, the [technical] improvement will enable population to grow, and will soon enable more people to live in misery than before.

The final result of [technical] improvements, therefore, is to increase the equilibrium population which is to increase the total sum of human misery."

To make us all happy he thought up his third theorem: "The moderately cheerful form of the Dismal Theorem"

"Fortunately, it is not too difficult to restate the Dismal Theorem in a moderately cheerful form, which states that if something else, other than misery and starvation, can be found which will keep a prosperous population in check, the population does not have to grow until it is

It is interesting that the hinterlands of the UK have changed. At one time all the vegetables, indeed most of the food that fed our cities, came from within a few miles of where the food was needed. For London this was mostly the land that now is occupied by Heathrow airport. Perhaps it is somewhat ironic that the food that now feeds the capital comes from all over the world, often via Heathrow airport.

The Urban Farmer

miserable and starves, and it can be stably prosperous."

Unfortunately we haven't found something else to take the place of misery. Misery is pretty good at limiting the population. But these days we not only have a situation where the numbers of people are going up, but the individuals in that population are also consuming more – behaving as though they are in fact more than one person themselves. For example, in the last ten years most Chinese have consumed as much as most Europeans, in fact now consuming as much as two or three of their countreparts in previous years.

And Now the Point – Where Is your Wealth?

Eventually, when you add up the effects of our economics and how we feed ourselves, our money economy will let us down. If more people are consuming more energy, food and resources, then to keep them happy we have to compete in a world economy that will out purchase what we in small western countries can afford. We see it already in energy. Are we not now at the mercy of oil production? We see it in the global food economy. When more want more, the biggest players will always get the lion's share.

So, where is your wealth? The bottom line is, biologically speaking, you are only as wealthy as the food you eat – and not the cost of it! If I earn a million pounds and live in a penthouse flat, how will I eat when my money has no value and I cannot buy it? Now I am not saying that the world is going to collapse into a morass of hopeless financial meltdown. But in the long run every person must become responsible for his own food, his own family on his own land – even if this land is a simple back garden at the back of a council house.

So The Urban Farmer's Handbook is all about that one thing, growing your own food because at some point in the future we all will need to do it – maybe not us, but maybe our children.

Why We Need Land Reform in the UK

There is a movement that has been gathering pace since the Second World War; that of Self-Sufficiency that more or less advocated "living the good life," growing your own and homemade cooking and food production. It has spawned half a dozen magazines, umpteen television programmes and a number of books. It is true that "of the writing of books there is no end" and this particular realm is full of them. To be honest you can go to any number of publications to get all the information you will ever need on how to look after hens or pigs or how to grow vegetables.

But there is a bigger need these days because the world has changed. We urgently need land reform in the UK and in many other western countries of the world to meet the needs of this changing world. Quite a mouthful, but there are lots of good reasons for it.

Economics

There is a huge pressure on ordinary people because of the changes in the world of business and money. We have become news dead over the years, but statistics which tell us that the current downturn is the worst in living memory should have a real impact on our thinking. For many thousands of families the future may be bleak. Jobs are being lost but people still need the ability to feed themselves.

It is the same economics that dictates from where we get our food in the world market. We had a plan to make the West a leader in a globalised economy. We would produce cars and drugs and various other high cost products and sell them around the world for food. This plan showed itself in the idea a recent government had to build houses all over the UK. It implied that we can house the population of the country in newly concreted fields and buy our food from Chile, Spain, New Zealand and anywhere else on the planet.

But the world isn't keeping its bargain. In the last seven years we have out consumed the world's farmers' ability to produce rice and wheat. For a few months in 2008 we in the West were only 50 days away from running out of wheat altogether. But even this isn't the full story. We have lived through a time of food riots, not in some land-locked African countries, but in Eastern Europe, Egypt and South America.

As the financial world spirals into ever decreasing turmoil, how do we expect to be able to pay for food in the world market? It stands to reason that those economies that have the biggest need and the greatest growth will outbid the rest of us when it comes to buying an ever diminishing cereal harvest. In the last year the UK economy shrunk by 0.5% whereas the Chinese grew by 8%, so whose population is going to be better fed in the long run?

Ecology and the F Word

It is no mistake that economics and ecology are actually the same word. They both represent housekeeping, the looking after the home, the pocket book of life, the life of money for economics and the life of living as far as ecology is concerned.

In real terms human ecology is the measure of the impact of every one of us on the planet and how the planet responds. After a long time of beating about the bush, not daring to use certain words, ecologists and economists are beginning to use the word famine and not in some far flung desert country where famine is a way of life, but in Brisbane, Sheffield and Lyon. The logic that brought us globalisation has brought with it serious consequences for the local food supply. As competition in a global market is now the way countries feed themselves there will inevitably be winners and losers. In the long run weakened currencies and the huge amounts that have had to be put into the paper money economy just to keep the system working and the fact that increasing numbers of people are all 'supping from the same pot' will mean that only the rich nations will be able to afford the better share of wheat and rice.

It is staples, the foods we rely on for our basic foodstuffs, that are the sharp focus here at the moment. China has lived for many generations on a rice and almost vegetarian diet. But things are changing in China. People who once lived a peasant lifestyle have tasted financial wealth and now require meat! The increase in beef, pork and chicken consumption in China is huge, and this has led to the grain bill also becoming much higher. The Chinese government, eager to show that the system works, has encouraged the market. China, with 20% of all the mouths to feed on the planet, is keen to consume more than their fair share almost as a badge of that success. The same goes for India and many of the emerging nations in Asia.

The financial side to human ecology, so far as it affects us in the

UK and Europe, is where, over the coming 10 to 20 years, we will find it harder to buy wheat because we will have been outbid by bigger and stronger economies. But what of the environmental side to human ecology?

Transport

The huge impact of transporting food around the world for financial gain is quite literally killing the planet. It is simple really. All transport between countries depends on oil, either for planes or ships. In the last hundred years we have released what took millions and millions of years of slow ecosystems to lay down. We have created an atmosphere more akin to the Jurassic era, in just 100 years. Delicately evolved systems of regulation are being smashed just so that we might eat food from around the world. And in our turn we produce more polluting industries and encourage emerging nations to do the same and get on the globalisation bandwagon.

Is this safe and how does it affect our food production?

In a speech at the Chatham House Conference titled "Food Security in the 21st Century" in 2008, the Rt. Hon Hilary Benn MP said:

"By 2050, there will be 9 billion of us sharing this fragile planet. That's the equal to adding another China and another India to the world in just over 40 years. Just think about that for a moment. It's why the FAO, World Bank and OECD estimate that global food production may need to double by 2050, but it will have to happen at a time when our climate is changing.

Farmers will have to cope with less reliable water supplies and increasingly frequent droughts and floods. So we will have to ensure that this huge increase in production is sustainable. And as well as adapting to climate change, the way we do agriculture will have to ensure that it does not add to the problem. Managing the land and the soil to lock in as much CO_2 as possible.

In short, we need to think about where and how we produce our food for the future."

He went on to say that in a changing financial world what seemed to be good ideas, such as the electronic identification of sheep, were no longer viable and that changes in the money system, such as

The Urban Farmer

For reasons of personal health, personal empowerment and the simple joy of growing, every person in every city needs the opportunity to grow at least some of their own food. In order to achieve this we need land reform. We need to be able to open up spaces in the city, even the city centre, so that people can grow vegetables and fruit. City centre allotments, however small, near homes and places of work will provide at least somewhere for people to grow. We need to be able to encourage land owners, industrialists and planners to free up land for people to grow food. How fantastic would it be if an allotment site was provided for in the planning application for new supermarkets and shopping centres and a number of plots made available for the people who worked in the area as well as the local residents?

the devaluation of the pound, increased prices. He also went on to say that our food supply was secure. Perhaps some years ago he would have said the same about the banking system, environmental change, increased world population and economies that must pollute to create the wealth they need in order to buy food are a fact of life.

Hilary Benn used his words carefully. He said that "of the food we could produce in this country, we are 74% self-sufficient." This figure sounds quite good, but looking behind the figures we have increased our food dependency on imported food by eightfold. We import 90% of our fruit and 50% of our vegetables. But it is the system behind the idea of global food production that is causing problems now and will continue to do so in the future. The idea is that nations find something they can grow better than anyone else and sell it. The money from this they then use to run their economies. This is a system headed for disaster, and indeed is producing serious problems. While this sentence is being written Atlantic Tuna is a few catches closer to extinction. The global demand for tuna is outstripping the ocean's ability to provide, but the need to earn money drives men to go out and get whatever there is out there.

The same goes for grassland for beef production around the world, where wholesale changes in ecosystems end up producing deserts. Almost every foodstuff traded on the world markets is now actually producing enormous ecological problems that are, in effect, depleting our ability to produce the very crop we set out to specialise in in the first place. The dependency of people on money, to produce a crop and sell it in order to survive, is creating dangerous situations. That money is now more important than the environment that gives life or the crop itself. This can only lead to enormous environmental problems.

Some of this is seen in the quality of soil around the world. In the UK we have a large amount of seriously degraded soil and much of the rest is in a poor state. But around the world agriculture loses between 5 and 10 million hectares every year because soil has changed enough to make its use impossible. This is an area roughly the size of England and Wales together.

The Rain It Raineth Every Day

In the UK we have had some great crops of wheat in recent years only to see it endangered by the wet summers we have experienced. This is a phenomenon predicted by scientists; as the greenhouse effect increases, so the weather will become increasingly erratic. Moreover, the ability of countries around the world to produce their own food will deteriorate. Take Afghanistan as an example. In 2006 there was a brilliant wheat crop which provided nearly 90% of their needs. However, in 2007 there was a drought that reduced this crop to almost nil. The country is now officially at risk and people are going hungry. This pattern repeated in countries around the world not only keeps cereal prices high, but makes the running of the political system increasingly problematic. Food security on a globalised scale is not achievable. There will always be hungry people and modern thinking says that it is only a matter of time before it is the industrialised nations of the world that have to bear the brunt.

We now realise that oil is running out so how will we drive our cars then? Well lets grow food and ferment the sugars to make alcohol? That'll do, won't it? Julian Cribb, Adjunct Professor of Science Communication at the University of Technology in Sydney and a Fellow of the Australian Academy of Technological Sciences and

The Urban Farmer

Engineering (ATSE), points out that the production of biofuel has tripled in the last five years, and that every acre now in production is another acre lost by agriculture to prop up industry.

Professor Cribb points to the demands on world agriculture in a very succinct way. The need is:

To increase farm production by 110 per cent using two thirds of the present water, three quarters of the present land area, with lower inputs of energy and fertiliser, with less new technology coming while facing increased drought & climatic uncertainty.

Everyone and anyone involved in the future planning of food production should realise that someone, somewhere is going to lose out. That indeed everyone will will eventually lose out and will have a diminished food supply. The social consequences of this will be grave indeed.

Food Should be Free – Land Reform

If I do my part I should hope that this planet of ours will sustain me. Indeed, experience says that it does, particularly in a climate that is neither too hot nor too cold, and has plenty of water. But I can hardly take advantage of it because I am poor, although in the west I am comparatively well off. I earn a wage and am probably, according to one of those poverty tracking websites, among the most wealthy 2% of the population on the planet. But in ecological terms I am poor. The recent banking fiasco and consequent downturn in the economy has shown me to be poor. If the state's ability to feed me suddenly diminished and if I wasn't able to go to the supermarket and buy bread for money, then I would have nothing to eat. A subsistence farmer is actually richer than I am even though I can buy a lot more things than he can, but he can grow his own food. Year in, year out, for generations, if all else remains the same, he can still grow food. The food I can grow in my little garden wouldn't last a month.

Associating allotments with schools would also be a wonderful way of integrating the growing public interest with school children. What a wonderful exercise this would be, not only in teaching children to grow, but also in working with older people, relationship building and naturally breaking down barriers.

Then we also need real land reform. Two hundred years ago William Cobbett wrote that the population of the land should expect to have an equal share in the goodness that comes from the land. If they worked hard they should be able to share in what the earth produced. To this end he famously said "A happy England is a pig in every yard." Now I am not allowed to keep a pig because I can't get a DEFRA number for it. Moreover, I cannot feed it swill because of foot and mouth regulations. I have to treat it just like any other pig farmer and buy all its food, or grow its food specially and separate from mine. I cannot even grow a row of carrots and give half of them to the pig and eat half myself.

The same goes for poultry and goats. But if it were possible for people who wanted to keep them to be trained in their care, and to be fairly sure that they would be legally able to keep them, then that would be land reform indeed.

In line with EU directives which are designed to encourage a global market,

John Seymour, the man who possibly more than anyone else started the current Home Farmer movement, said: "I am only one. I can only do what one can do. But what one can do, that I will do." It's OK talking about city centre spaces and urban farms, but everyone's homes and gardens, their walls and their streets and any green spaces are available for the growing of food. These spaces are more than just growing zones. They are for learning and teaching, for social inclusion, for taking school children and for including everyone in the growing of their own food.

the abattoir provision in this country is abysmal. In some counties they do not exist at all and you are faced with a journey of 50 or more miles in order to have your animals killed legally. We need local abattoirs and local markets and the ability to buy and prepare our own animals. Then, more than anything else, we need education.

To be realistic, you cannot embark on urban farming with just a bucket of feed in one hand and an instruction book in the other. We need to make it possible for people to learn how to do it; how to love and cherish their fruit, vegetables and livestock and how to grow wheat – just imagine an inner city swathe of wheat! And more than anything else we need a cultural change where people grow up wanting to grow their own food, where they value poultry and livestock and home produced food like cheese and bread more than computer games and some of the city's current attractions. Then the city would begin to look green – but this is a bit more than land reform!

The Way Forward

First of all we should allow communities to take responsibility for their own food production. It sounds scary, but in the long run this is such an important step. If the economics of food production do happen to go the way the worst scenarios have predicted, then with community responsibility for the production of food it will matter far less if the government finds it can can no longer feed the population? At least local communities will have a say about what happens to the land and can arrange the growing of food so that everyone gets a fair share.

To an extent the provision of allotments already has a measure of local control, but the provision of more land, of more spaces in city centres, around schools and in as many imaginative places as we can find is an important provision for the future.

I recently had a meeting with the chief planner for the city centre of Manchester. They are proud of their city centre in Manchester. The plan has been to convert parking bays and loose land anywhere in the city to allow people to grow their own food. The Manchester centre population has risen to over 20,000 in recent years from a figure of just 5 in the early 1990s, one a Coronation Street actress, Pat Phoenix, living in a town centr hotel and the others caretakers. But there isn't anywhere for these people to grow any of their own food. A raised bed, a rubbish skip or even some rubble sacks are all that would be required for people to grow some vegetables. A roof top would be fine for bees and a yard for chickens – in fact anywhere that is free and accessible would be great.

"But do you know the capital value of a parking bay in the city?" The planner who provided the above information on city centre residents, who also happens to be an old friend, took a sip of his coffee in the very swish Art Gallery cafe in which we sat. "Three million pounds." Three million pounds for a piece of land no bigger than a car. Somehow we need to get beyond money, and in order to do this we need either a change in culture or alternatively government involvement in order to help free up land in the city.

But it goes beyond just having land; being able to use it is another thing. Much of our industrial wasteland is not fit to grow crops for human consumption. I often travel into Manchester on an urban train and what was once busy train tracks is now a complete wasteland, a huge acreage of oil soaked and unusable land, but it could be reclaimed to provide growing places, safe from the remaining trains. The same goes for the unused bridges, the vacant factory plots and the weed ridden car parks that encircle the city.

Much of this land is owned by someone. On the whole they are waiting for an upturn in business so that the value of their resource can increase. Maybe someone could build a new factory, a new housing estate or a new road? But this hope does not necessilary exclude people from growing crops. It is neither expensive nor difficult to devise a series of allotment spaces that people could use and which could be moved somewhere else at the end of the season. A two tonne rubble sack can grow a remarkable amount of potatoes but when emptied of compost it can be folded up and carried away to a new site.

The use of local authority recycled compost is more than adequate to provide growing materials and, though not truly organic, it still remains an excellent resource and, should a site be needed for building or other purposes, the compost can then be used in the landscaping.

There are already a number of models around the UK for community gardens and urban growing. These isolated, though extremely important and innovative projects, need to become the norm for every city. Planning is an important part of all this. The tallest building in Manchester took just ten weeks to get through planning, but if I wanted to build an allotment on some waste ground in the city I wouldn't mind betting it would take much longer. This doesn't mean that planners are nasty, anti-green people – far from it. They just need the political impetus that values urban growing, and this can be translated into action on the ground. Like most things, the key to changing the way we do things is to find the people behind the people who are responsible for decision making.

Recently, near where I live in the city, youths set fire to some buildings housing horses. The unfortunate animals died and there was an outcry. It turned out that the children responsible were already in care and out of control. I would wager that these children, if given the chance to look after livestock themselves, could work closely with and build relationships with other people looking after livestock. They would also never have done such a thing in the first place. There is a lot more at stake here than food.

Introduction Part 3
The Importance of Security

The ordinary farmer who lives away from the town must have good fences to keep his animals from escaping, and even when they do escape there is rarely any harm done and stock is usually recovered with only a minor inconvenience. But when you live in the town you have to ensure that your stock is also safe from the outside world. The same goes for your crops, your equipment and utensils.

But it's not just a case of keeping people out. Keeping your stock in has a double importance in the town. First of all there are more opportunities for them to cause damage to themselves or to other people's property. Secondly, it is important to make sure that your animals are not seen as a nuisance to your neighbours. I feel it is important that in order to successfully run a self-sufficient urban garden-farm, you will need to have your stock as invisible and unnoticed as possible. The less anyone can see of your activities the better.

The third reason for the highest security is to keep predators out, both human and otherwise. Urban foxes are so bold as to come along in daylight and simply kill your chickens without eating them. Losses to foxes far outweigh human attacks and there are always cats of all kinds ready to take poultry and dogs ready to stress your animals, if not kill and eat them.

Animal droppings are an even bigger problem, especially when you are trying to grow salads, but poultry and pigs are affected by dog mess, pigeon mess and what not.

Feed security is of the utmost importance. Tidiness and security make for a feed store that excludes rats, and this is the biggest problem for any urban situation. Neighbours fear rats more than anything else and no amount of explaining that there is no reason for them to worry, or that rats are everywhere, or that rats are actually quite clean animals will make any difference. The effect is the same – you will have the environmental health people knocking on your door before you know it.

Pest and disease security is an important consideration in small area farming. For example, you might have hens in a run allowing them to scratch and dig without much of a problem, leading a happy life as hens should. But the build up of parasites in the soil will eventually cause them to become sick, and any new stock infected. The normal response to this is to have a regime of moving the birds to fresh land giving the soil a chance to recover. However, this is not always possible where space is at a premium. Keeping poultry on concrete with some spent compost sprinkled on top, with a box of earth for

The Urban Farmer

them to scratch in, is a viable alternative. This way the run can be cleaned regularly, parasites swept away and the hens kept healthy.

Similarly, make it a golden rule never to walk on your soil. Crop diseases are spread through the plot by feet. You can hardly ever find an allotment site that doesn't have clubroot spread by a thousand feet plodding all over the place.

The very best security to be had is supplied by plants. They take up room for sure but if you can get an impenetrable hedge, people will not come through it. Plants will also hide the site from prying eyes and deaden sounds galore. They are also good to look at and have the advantage, if you choose the right ones, of being edible.

However, hedges will not be enough on their own if you want to keep cats and foxes out of the site. The easiest way to deter urban cats is to keep a dog, but this merely brings different problems. There are few other ways of doing it. I have seen cats walk, albeit gingerly, between the nails of a fence designed to keep people out. Foxes are another matter altogether. You can make a fence behind the hedge, but make sure it is both stout and tall.

Electric fences are useful only where you have enough room to keep them away from things that might short them out. Pigs especially soon learn that if they push their trough to the fence they will short it out and they can then set off on a spending spree to the local shops, possibly taking in the odd pub or two on the way home.

Fencing for urban farmers takes on a greater importance than for the ordinary farmer; in fact his life is dominated by fencing. The point is simple; the consequences of any livestock running around the housing estate is a million times greater than the same animals running around the countryside. John Seymour bought a farm in Wales and there were no fences at all. Other farmers' animals came onto John's land and even into his house. Similarly his horse escaped and they eventually found it some five miles away. Imagine five miles from an urban garden – your animals might even be on the town hall steps!

The urban farmer has to have good fences, but they must also be good looking ones to boot, something the rest of the farming world might even laugh at. Remember that a waney lapp wooden fence is completely useless against any kind of onslaught. Even chickens can get through them and as soon as the winter arrives they tend to blow away anyway. So make sure your fence is appropriate to your animals and keep them up to scratch all of the time.

Security from and for the Neighbours

The biggest problem you are going to have if you are to set about urban farming will come from the neighbours.

The thought of having a complete loonie next door who keeps hens, and possibly worse, is often too much for some people.

The thought of having someone next door who might kill their animals for food can also be enough turn a normally peaceful neighbourly relationship into an all out war. When I told my neighbour that I was going to keep bees their daughter literally packed her bags to leave home. In the end I kept my bees in a factory just over the road without them even knowing and they were never once troubled by them – or even knew they were there.

Take it slowly. Give them your produce to enjoy but keep your plans to yourself. This is the best way of keeping people happy. If my neighbour thought I was going to keep hens the first thing they would say is "Rats?" And if I was to say I was keeping hens while my garden is a complete quagmire, they would worry about what came next. But keeping a tight ship, with every possible problem catered for and the odd box of eggs, will keep most people onside. The urban farmer has to be both neat and tidy, without causing smells or residues. There must never be any hint of nuisance and you should ooze confidence that all is well. Chickens and ducks should never be allowed over the fence, goats should be trouble free and pigs should be secure and perfectly good tempered!

Jersey

Dexter

Highland

Chapter One

The Urban Cow

I haven't enough room for a cow. At one time a hundred years ago Mr. Bill Salt lived in Newton Heath. He lived in a house that was falling down and he had no running water. His wife and children worked in the mill by the canal that is now an office block. He had no garden, just a yard. But he did have an allotment. The allotment is still there but it bears needles and rusting bicycles instead of cabbages. And he had a cow. Many people had cows – they were kept on the common that was owned by the Deacons of the Cathedral in Manchester. Bill Salt was better off than I am today – I have no room for a cow! The common was sold to the council for a housing estate and what remained in the hands of the Deacons became an illegal tip. The land is now so polluted that the teachers at the local school could not breathe the air when the rain forced the polluted water off the tip and into the drains.

If you look at the city from the air there is plenty of green. Indeed, where I live, nestled between the motorway, the canal and the factories, a farm used to have cattle. Now it just keeps horses because their £30 a week pays more than the cattle and an army of young girls feed and groom and pamper the animals. But there are fields where cattle could be kept if necessary. Such an animal could be shared by a number of families and they could use the meat, the milk and possibly more importantly the manure the cow produces. A milk yield of four gallons would be adequate for as many as 16 – 20 families, and there could be enough left over for cheese and other dairy products. And on top of this there is a calf every year too!

On average you need an acre of land for a cow, but this figure belies the fact that the majority of cattle are kept in large herds. In order not to dry up and run out of milk you do need two cows. Since the animal needs a lot of hay in the winter – a good tonne, then you need the better part of an acre just for this. The animal would need to be housed for at least a part of the winter, just to keep up the condition of the soil. And keeping the fertility of the soil, and therefore the quality of the grass, in good order would be very difficult. So the minimum amount of land you would need to be comfortable would be 2 acres of easily fenced land. You could section off a half acre to make hay in the summer and possibly get three quarters of your requirement. You could fertilise the land with composted manure and more easily cope with her progeny when they appear.

This is not garden farming, but it can still be urban farming. Let's be honest, you can't read a general chapter about keeping cows in a book on urban farming and expect to know enough to keep them successfully. You couldn't do that even from the greatest encyclopaedia on cattle. This chapter is about giving you the impetus, should you be able to put together the necessary requirements. So if I have been able to whet your appetite, find someone who keeps cattle and stick to him like glue for a few weeks.

Cattle security

Cows do not like dogs and they like the mess that dogs leave behind even less. Thankfully most dogs don't like cattle either, but your fencing should be completely dog proof. It isn't a bad idea to keep some geese in the same field too because they will be aggressive with intruders and even people walking by. If possible keep your cow shed – if you need one for winter, in a very private place, preferably near the house in a very well fenced area. Only move your cattle around at times when they will not draw attention to themselves and try to make your fences secure so that anyone who might get into the field would worry about how they might get out. A self locking high gate that is difficult to climb and padlocked is a must. Perhaps the best fencing is wooden with a hedge growing in it, making it difficult to see over the top.

Feeding

Unlike horses, cattle will not just go to anyone for food and will happily munch away as long as the grass is good quality. Grass growth is dependent firstly on temperature, secondly on water and finally on nutrients. In October the metabolism of grass changes and it reduces nutrient uptake, although it might still be growing. Winter grass is not as good quality as summer grass. Your cow will maintain its basic needs and have enough to produce milk on grass alone in the summer, but will require a top up in the winter of hay and concentrates. And since most cattle are kept indoors in the winter for the sake of the grass, you may find yourself feeding the cow artificially until the late spring.

Put all the feed into a feeder which keeps it clean and uncontaminated and stops the animal from treading all over the food.

On average a cow will eat 2% of its weight of dry matter each day. This can increase by another 1% if it is cold and another if it is milking. This translates to 5 kg grain a day, with a similar amount of straw available and plenty of water. If you are feeding hay you could be using as much as 10 – 15 kg and if you are topping up with roots – carrots, mangles, swedes and so on you should consider 10 - 15 Kg as a good addition to 10 Kg good hay. You will get a good idea about the quality of the food because it will be reflected in the condition of the animal, the milk yield and the greediness of the animal.

The Urban Farmer

It might seem inappropriate to have to follow certain regulations clearly designed for large organisations, but without the correct clarification from the department you must follow all the rules or face a huge inconvenience, a fine or even a criminal record. So before you even think of urban cattle, get the current information and get help.

Breeds

It is amazing the number of smallholders who keep Dexter cattle, so much so that it is often called 'The Smallholder's Cow.' They are small and good all-rounders and have the benefit of being a little flighty. The ones I have known have, at times, been downright bad tempered, just the kind of animal to deter any attention from the locals. They also give enough milk for a few families and the meat is brilliant.

Much has already been written about the Jersey. Certainly they are pretty, they have excellent milk – possibly the best milk, and they are small. They are a little expensive to buy and they do not have much in the way of good meat.

John Seymour said that the Jersey bull, opposed to the cow who is a darling, is 'a little sod.' So beware.

The larger breeds and the traditional ones such as Aberdeen Angus or Holstein Fresian are just not suited to small acreages and I would keep away from them. Of course there are always exceptions, and in particular the Highland seems to suit the small fields and the regime of the urban situation and they will do fine outside at any time of the year.

Housing

After some seriously distressing occurrences in the inner city with horses and other animals, I would prefer a cow shed to be made of hollow concrete blocks with a concrete floor and a steel roof. The feed could be locked inside out of the way and reach of idiots who light fires and I would prefer to see a smoke alarm in the shed and a large, dangerous looking dog outside.

Inside the shed should have a space that is at least one and a half times the length of the animal all round, so it can move easily and another space for its offspring of similar proportions. You will need room for your kit and food and you will also need water. You can deep litter a cow easily by simply layering fresh straw on top of the old and cleaning this out in the spring which is not too smelly or disgusting and it makes the best compost in the world.

The animal needs constant and liberal amounts of fresh water, usually provided from a drinker fed from the mains and there should be food available at head height.

Breeding

Anyone keeping cattle in an urban situation will do well not to keep a bull but use Artificial Insemination (AI). We will talk a lot about artificial insemination in relation to pigs. When you see your animal is ready you should have the materials to hand. You will know that the animal is ready if she is excessively noisy or starts to mount her sisters, should you have them. She will also have discharge from her hind quarters. If you only have one animal you might as well stand the expense and get someone in to check. AI centres are dotted around the country, though you might find it difficult to get rare breed semen. The technique of AI for cattle can be learned, and will take a few days of instruction and "hands on" experience. In order to make it work you need to find the cervix, then enter via the anus and guide the gun to the three necked entrance to the womb and then, whilst still having one hand in the intestine, manoeuvre the nozzle through the three layered neck and into the womb itself, where you then inject the semen. It is a lot to ask of a novice, and unless you can justify the expense of learning and keeping up to date with the subject, you might as well buy in a man to do the job. (No pun intended)

The Urban Farmer

Milking a Cow

First of all you need to be prepared: a pail, a short stool, two hands and a very gentle milk cow are all you need to enjoy fresh milk every day. Once you start milking your cow she will have to be milked twice a day every day at the same time until you let her dry up. Routine is everything here. You must also sit on the same side of the cow as well.

Place your stool at a right angle to the cow and sit with your head resting on her flank. Wash her udder with warm water and a clean cloth and place the pail under the teats.

Now take a teat into the palm of your hand and squeeze it at the top with your thumb and forefinger. Continue squeezing each finger around the teat, forcing the milk in a stream until allyour fingers are around the teat.

Release the teat.

Repeat until only a small amount of milk comes out and the udder is soft to the touch.

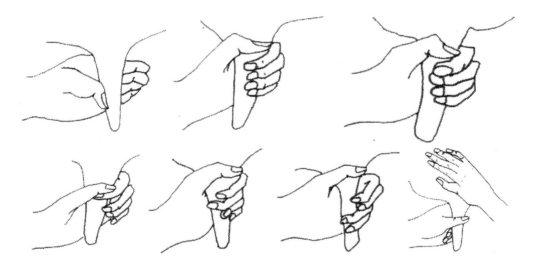

Getting Ready

Cows spend about nine months in labour and during the last six weeks they can be under fed a little. I have to say that I have never yet experienced a cow needing any help in birthing. You leave them one night and in the morning there is a little calf. I once had a cow making a terrible row at 2.00am and I ran out to see her, but the calf was there lying on the floor. She was just saying her prayers.

It is best to leave them for a good few hours in labour before you worry about them, but if your experience is limited, get some help. Get to know another cow man that knows what he is doing and for the cost of a few pints will give you the help you need. Better still, attend as many births as you can once your animal is pregnant. And if this is your first time, get hold of a good vet. You are not paying him to do the job, but to teach you. Knowledge is always worth paying for.

If she births in a field, pick the calf up and allow her to sniff you and it together and walk slowly to the byre where they can stay together for a few days at least. To get the best of starts the calf should have all its mother's milk for at least a week.

Unless you sell the calf at a week old the best regime for the urban farmer is what John Seymour calls 'single-suckling.' In other words, run the calf with its mother in the field until it is six months old and then sell, unless you want to keep her. If it is a bull then you are much better getting it to market.

If you want all of her milk then you need to get the calf off its mother at a month or so and feed it yourself. The young calf will take half of her milk and when you first separate them mum will make a dreadful fuss but within a week you wouldn't know they were related.

A calf will take a gallon of milk a day from day one leading up to a gallon and a half by the end of the month, and at this time it can be slowly weaned off milk. You can feed the animal on concentrates, around 2kg a day plus as much grass as it wants. If you can manage it, a situation where you are able to milk mum while the calf also has access to the teat is the easiest and most successful management situation, especially if they are both outside.

Officialdom

In order to keep cattle at all you have to register as a holding first. If you are truly urban you should expect trouble. You will be assessed for the suitability of the land, the access, people and other users of the area on which you are trying to keep livestock, the effects of your farming on water courses and the potential for nuisance and disease problems. Your land will have to be adequate in size for the animals you are proposing to keep and the official will be keen to assess if you can afford the cost of fences and their upkeep because the consequences of an escapee animal can be very serious for the general public. You will also be assessed on the provision, storage and transport of both food and water. And finally you will have to have plenty of insurance. The NFU will help with that.

I once had a cow charge into a caravan, making the door much wider than it was designed to be and, although the cow was as gentle as you would wish in the field, in the caravan she was a demon, so you will understand that urban farms are completely different to country ones.

Once you have your holding number you can then apply for a password and account with the British Cattle Movement Scheme, which is a computerised cattle tracing system and you will have to get your cattle passport from DEFRA. You can get all the information on the current regulations by looking at the Cattle Keeper's Handbook from the Rural Payments Agency. Every keeper of cattle should have this and it is freely available either online at http://www.rpa.gov.uk or from DEFRA.

Cattle Problems

As soon as you register cattle, even a lone cow on a lone standing, you will trigger DEFRA to test this animal for TB. Bovine TB is a terrible problem if you are going to drink raw milk or eat raw cheese. Should your animal have TB then it will be culled, and you will get compensation, though certainly not enough to encourage you to get more cattle.

The list of diseases to which cattle can succumb will scare you to death. Healthy feeding is important, as is a good shelter from driving rain. You should keep your field clean of harmful weeds such as ragwort and keep them wormed regularly. A salt lick is packed with trace elements and any water running into the field should be consistently clean.

There are many books on cattle husbandry and veterinary care, but the real place to learn is beside someone who has kept cattle all their lives, so before you decide on cattle, get help, get information and take your time.

There are many who will immediately balk at keeping a single cow in a confined space, and an acre is a confined space for a cow, and probably rightly so – but the urban farmer might well feel, and economics one day might dictate, that people in cities really do need to keep cattle.

Good Points in a Goat

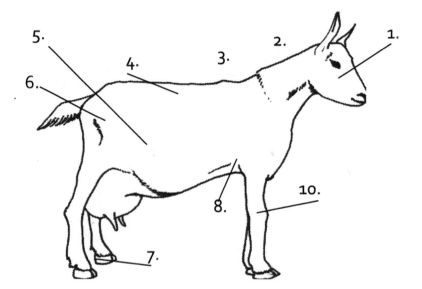

1. Shapely and intelligent head, 2. Long neck, 3, Neat shoulders, 4. Long and level back, 5. Deep and well sprung ribs, 6. wide pelvis, 7. Sound and neat feet, 8. deep body, 10. straight forelegs.

Chapter Two

The Urban Goat

There is a debate among experts about the nature of Mediterranean flora. I remember my old professor telling me that the feral goat ate its way around North Africa and the Middle East, leaving the landscape bare of grass and shrubs. I believed this until I spoke to a lady who ran a charity dedicated to providing goats to African families. She told me there were a lot of goats there because they were the only animals able to survive on such a meagre scrub.

Whichever way you look at it, goats do turn food into good-quality meat and milk and they are a great deal more efficient than cattle in doing so. But it has to be said that the old adage about computers – 'rubbish in, rubbish out' – holds true. If you are thinking of keeping goats at all you shouldn't imagine that they can be kept on poor rations.

If you like the milk, a pair of goats is probably better for the smallholder than a cow because they are more efficient at converting food to milk and you do not have so much milk to deal with at any one time. The smallest yield of milk from a cow is many times that from a goat.

The Urban Farmer

Keeping Goats

You have to realise from the outset the facts of life. If you want a goat to give milk, it must first be mated and produce offspring. Then the animal will give milk and another goat (or three). The problem is that they have a propensity to produce male goats, so be prepared and understand what you may have to do with them. You will find it all but impossible to sell them, even dressed in a diamond tiara.

Near where I live, in the urban part of north Manchester, there is a field by a bend in the heavily polluted River Irk. The field is bordered by a canal, the railway and the river and I dare say it will become a housing estate in due course. At the moment around two dozen goats live in the field. They are out in all weathers and brave the wet and snow with equal resilience. But there is a world of difference between having an almost wild set of animals and some goats for personal use.

> If you think you can keep goats in a nice lawned garden and all will be well, think again.

Not only will your plants and shrubs, including the roses, disappear into the animal, you will also find that the grass will soon start to resemble a battlefield – especially if the weather continues in its current trends. Also you will find your animals will begin to have hoof problems. Consequently, goats are just as happy, if not more so, being kept on concrete. It is much easier to clean and can be kept comparatively free of parasites.

Goats really do need housing at night and protection from the rain, which makes them go downhill more than anything else. They need a copious supply of water and good food and they are better with a partner than alone. They need to be attended for at least part of each half day just in case they get into trouble, which is far from unusual. In the urban setting they will need very good fencing and they shouldn't be left alone tethered. If you do tether them they need a swivel joint on the leash to prevent knotting.

Regulations

If you want to keep a goat, even a small pigmy goat as a pet, you need a CPH (County, Parish, Holding) number which is issued by DEFRA. This might prove difficult because if you only have a garden they will come along and check you out and look at access and the impact on the area etc. If, however, the local council don't mind the keeping of livestock on your allotment, then you are much more likely to be successful. Once you have a holding number it is easier to keep pigs and other livestock.

With a holding number you can go ahead and buy your goats! You will be issued with a herd number and you will need to keep careful records of animal movements and outcomes etc. All goats need to be ear tagged to comply with animal movement regulations.

Breeds

There are dozens of types of goats, some milkers, others for meat, some all-rounders, some pets, some even used as draught animals to pull a cart.

British Toggenburg

This is a milker that produces quality and quantity with a good length of lactation. It is a well-mannered goat and is easy to keep and control. There are few health problems associated with them and they produce around 3 litres (6 pints) of milk a day.

How to Buy

By far the best way to buy goats is to get involved with a local club and spend some time alongside people who know about them. There are goat clubs around the country but the best one to make contact with is the British Goat Society, which has an excellent website packed with helpful information. The society will give you the details of a local breeder or member who will be happy to show you the ropes.

The Urban Farmer

Anglo Nubian

Please don't get me wrong – I like them. The Anglo Nubian has a prop forward's face, a bit like mine. The nose is full and is sometimes described as 'Roman' but I have never seen a Roman with a face like that. The breed society describes it as having 'a high, proud head carriage and majestic bearing.' It is a good breeding animal that produces slightly smaller quantities of very rich milk. It is the ideal goat for cheese making.

Saanen

This goat comes from Switzerland and is creamy white – camouflage against all that snow! This is a good all rounder that produces a lot of milk and good meat. I have to say the mildest tempered, kindest animal I ever knew was a Saanen. We used to sit and chat together in the mornings and then when she was fed up with my conversation she would tap me on the arm politely and wander off.

Golden Guernsey

Much sought after and much loved, Golden Guernseys in the UK have been developed from goats orginally imported from the Channel Islands. They are raised for milk but do not produce as much as the larger dairy breeds. Butterfat and protein levels are generally the same as in most other breeds.

They are considered the ideal 'urban' goat as they are suitable for those without grazing who have a very small plot of land and want to give their family wholesome milk produced at home.

Feeding Goats

The British Goat Society produces a good booklet called 'Goat Feeding,' which sets out daily routines and rations for various breeds at various weights and so on.

Of course, as with all animals, newborn goats should be allowed complete access to their mother so they get the benefit of the colostrum in her initial lactation. A perfectly workable system for mum, kids and yourself is to allow the kid to run with mum all day. This way they can have all the milk they want during the day. Separate them at night and before you allow them to run out together, milk mum. She will replace what you have taken and have a supply available for the kid in a short while.

You can separate them completely if you can stand the noise and then the kids will need bottle feeding until they are three months old. They start on around 400ml four times a day and peak at around 800ml three times a day at eight weeks, gradually reducing to around 400ml a day by 12 weeks and after that they are on solid food.

By far the most important feed is hay with grass and other forage thrown in ad lib. You can also feed a supplemental goat mix of grain and sugar beet. The average goat will munch its way through 0.5kg (1.1lb) of hay, 5kg (11lb) of grass and 1kg (2.2lb) of goat mix daily.

Salt licks should be available that give the goats a lot of minerals.

Milking

This is a remarkably simple thing. On the whole goats like it as much as the humans. You need to get them onto a stand to make it comfortable for yourself. I made one from a pile of pallets with the goat tethered and offered some food.

Please be good mannered enough to warm your hands and clean the udders with a surgical wipe. If the teats are tender or express blood she might have mastitis and need some attention.

The actual process of milking has to be learned. It is not easy at first, but you will be surprised how tough the teat is. You are making a wave with your fingers, squeezing and pulling slightly as you continue to close the fingers around the teat.

You will feel the udder chamber emptying, and you should go round them evenly and collect all the milk.

The Urban Farmer

It is not unusual for a goat keeper to spend the whole day with a sick animal, cajoling talking and simply petting.

I have used Yoghurt (natural - not strawberry flavour!) as I have found it to be a brilliant way of bringing a sick goat - particularly one that has had tummy problems - back to health.

Problems

The fundamental rule is that they should not be left alone if tethered and they should never, repeat never, be left with a collar. They are extraordinarily good at killing themselves.

Many goat problems come on gradually and need you to observe them closely. Get to know your animals, watching how they eat and when and how much and how they drink and relate to other members of the herd and, of course, obvious things like milk yield, stool consistency and the colour and smell of their urine.

A goat that is feeling poorly will likely as not just lie on the ground and not move at all when you approach it. This is quite unusual because they often come to greet you with a smile. A sick goat is a little like a sick child except that the goat is much more prone to simply giving up. An ill animal needs to be separated from the herd and you will need to spend time with it, stroking, looking for tenderness, bloating, cud coming from the mouth, runny or dry eyes and so on.

Once the diagnosis has been made, mostly if not exclusively by the vet, you need to get stuck in to nursing.

It is not unusual for a goat keeper to spend the whole day with a sick animal, cajoling, talking and simply petting. I have found yoghurt to be a brilliant way of bringing a sick goat, particularly one that has had tummy problems, back to health.

Tempting the animal with food, and you'll get to know what it likes, is another way of keeping the will to live alive.

You will have to get used to caring for your animal's feet - trimming the hoof and watching for excess growth. They will also need regular worming, but be careful not to over do it because you can get resistant strains of parasites that no wormer can shift.

If you have any grazing at all try to keep them on grass that has not had goats on it in the previous year and keep them off the grass until summer when parasite eggs and lavae have died.

Goats are great fun, and yes, you can keep them in urban situations if you have the extra security for their safe keeping. The best 'next step' would be to find your nearest goat keeper and tag along to learn the ropes.

Gloucestershire Old Spot

Berkshire

Oxford Sandy and Black

Chapter Three

The Urban Pig

In 1822 William Cobbett wrote that a happy England was a pig in every yard. Why did he say this when it sounds to modern ears such a strange thing to say? At the time Great Britain was going through all sorts of changes. Machines had taken over individual men's skills and almost the whole population was being forced off the land. They were losing the right to keep animals on common land and the poor could not even take rabbits that were eating crops or pigeons that sat under the railway bridges. The poor were landless people who had to work for ever reducing wages and buy food from shops that were owned by the people who gave them their wages in the first place.

In 1823 England was very close to revolution and to counter it every landowner had to keep a militia ready to subdue the poor. They managed it too, once or twice in various northern towns where soldiers killed a few as a way of making the rest realise their place. Strong stuff, but what has this to do with keeping pigs these days? Well, Cobbett was saying that every family in the country had the right to live off the fullness which the land could

The Urban Farmer

Training

We will say, time and again, that you cannot keep pigs with a book in one hand and a pig in the other. This chapter is basically to whet the appetite, to make you feel as though you will be able to keep pigs in the first place. The very best thing you can do is invest some money in a pig course which will give you the opportunity to handle pigs, to get over your nervousness and see if they really are for you.

provide, which was a bit of a radical thing to say. He affirmed the rights of everyone to keep a pig.

Now is not the time or place to start up a new 'pig revolution' for land reform but needless to say, the urban farmer has got his work cut out if he is going to keep pigs in his garden at all. Getting a holding number and keeping the paperwork on track is no mean task. But let us assume that you have the right permissions and you are able to keep pigs properly.

The Garden Pig

It doesn't exist! But I do hope that this can be brought about - Oh! how we need land reform in this country.

People often think that keeping pigs involves a breeding sow and a great fit boar to service her. The urban farmer might find this too difficult a task because of the space needed for the sow and her piglets. However, buying weaners, pigs at 8 weeks old, already used to taking dry food is probably the best bet. They will be ready for slaughter in seven months.

The first thing to realise when keeping pigs is that they are intelligent animals. They need friends and attention and plenty to do. There are other problems with this intelligence; they are brilliant escapees. They quickly learn that if you kick your feeding tray onto an electric fence it stops working and then you can leg it without being shocked. They learn the difference between a waney lap fence, through which they will simply walk into next door's garden, and a good strong fence. They will remember exactly what time you feed them and make a terrible fuss if you are late.

The other thing about pigs is that because they are intelligent, you get to like them, and then you begin to wonder about killing and eating a sentient animal and you have to be sure about what you are doing in your own mind.

For me it is a simple question. Do I like eating pork and bacon? Why do I like eating pork and bacon and is this desire any different to why a lion likes eating gazelles? If no then I feel I am morally right to keep a pig for food. But I know this logic does not work for everyone. What I am left with is the moral question of whether I can be absolutely sure I can give this animal a brilliant piggy life.

Breeds

Pigs are big, sometimes really big! They start off sweet, playful and there is nothing as satisfying as watching piglets playing tag on a summer's day - great fun. But by the age of 14 weeks they are like unruly teenagers.

Once upon a long time ago (only fifty years ago, actually) practically each county had its own breed of pig; the Essex Pig, the Wessex Pig, the small Yorkshire and so on. This gave rise to regional sausages such as the Cumberland, but that is another story.

There has, thanks to the smallholder movement, been a revival of the traditional breeds such as the Gloucestershire Old Spot, the Tamworth, the Berkshire and the Oxford Sandy and Black in the last 5 years and their numbers, whilst still small and on the rare breed at risk list, are increasing once more.

Gloucestershire Old Spots

Sometimes called The Orchard Pig the GOS is the oldest spotted pedigree breed in the world. They are placid and easily managed - a most laid back pig which makes them ideal for the first time pig keeper. They are also tough and hardy making them suitable for rearing outdoors.

The Urban Farmer

Oxford Sandy and Blacks

Traditionally an outdoor pig used to running free in woodlands, rough grazing and pasture. It is a multi-purpose breed producing succulent pork, fine bacon & excellent ham. Like the GOS they are an ideal breed for the beginner as they are docile and easily handled.

Housing

Pigs need to have a sturdy home. They are at their best in a pig ark kept on grass.

> In an urban situation you have to remember that the pig can run for a long way at a pace that humans cannot match.

So if you keep them loose you need to be sure that they are securely fenced in, and that people and dogs are securely fenced out.

A pig ark is made from wood and corrugated iron and must be strong enough to be knocked about by its rowdy inhabitants. All they will need is some straw to sleep on. They never muck in the ark, so are very clean and easy to deal with. The ark can be moved from one part of a field to another as pigs are really good at digging and will turn the field to mud in no time. Another way of looking at it is to simply appreciate that they are probably the most brilliant ploughs you can buy. They manure the soil, grow fat on the plants they root out, they will if allowed, produce their own replacements and finally you can eat them.

Once treated to pigs the land is in good heart and ready for a crop. All you need to do is to rake it or harrow it if large and then plant up.

You will read of all kinds of housing being available for pigs, some made from straw and others from old tyres and various hacked together buildings. In my opinion the urban farmer will always have a problem of credibility; unless it looks right you will be in danger of attracting the wrath of the various people in the neighbourhood. I would try to avoid home-made housing of any kind unless you are completely sure of doing a more than excellent job.

Feeding

Pigs are not good eaters. Well actually they are, but it is surprising how they over eat, or how poorly they digest their food and how easily they go off it. Unfortunately, since we have such amazingly difficult laws, you are not allowed to feed pigs food that has been grown for human consumption.

> You can no longer give them your scraps from your plate, or even share a biscuit with them in the morning with a cup of tea. Theoretically you cannot take an egg from the kitchen and give it as a snack to the pig, something I have done many a time. They eat the lot including the shell.

It has to be said that growing pigs means you have to buy in pig meal and you won't get into that much bother by giving the animal the odd treat. If you have any thoughts about selling your animal, however, you will have to stick to the rules like glue.

Pig pellets are made from a combination of barley, wheat middles and fish meal. Much depends on the age of the pig and feed can get quite confusing. You can buy early pellets for weaners for pigs 4 – 8 weeks old and growers for those above this. Then, if you have a breeding sow, you can get breeder's mixture. They come in 25kg bags and should be stored

Pigs can be very greedy and fight to consume as much food as they can. The pecking order, or should I say 'let's all have a violent fight around the trough order', can be quite difficult. I have had pigs that have needed to be separated during feeding times by a careful manipulation of doors and fences.

where rats and mice cannot get to them. The trick is not to buy too much in one go.

The point is not to over feed them. As a general rule you should feed half a kilo of pellets per month of the animal's age up to a maximum of about 3 kilos. They will find all sorts of ways of telling you they are hungry and if they get too fat, they will turn away from their food. So it's a case of judging what you feel is good and if the weather is cold you might find they need more food or less if it is seriously hot. I usually feed them twice a day.

They should always have water in a container they cannot kick over. You can guarantee they will kick it over if possible, just for the fun of it.

Remember that pigs are omnivores. They eat anything really and are the gourmets of the farm. Keep them happy with a series of different types of tit bits, some salad thrown over the fence, the odd apple or some pellets thrown around so they have to hunt them out.

Moving Pigs

I once watched a child moving a pig in a competition. The animal simply wouldn't do what the boy wanted and so he got cross. He was using a pig stick, somewhat more like a whip than a stick, and a board. The basic idea is to let the pig walk down an imaginary corridor by using the board and gently moving the pig with the stick. The further the pig went away from the frustrated child the harder he whacked it. Pretty soon there was a weald on the pig's shoulder and it was getting worse. In the end the boy threw both the board and the stick at the pig and ran off crying. The pig retreated to the corner of the ring and had a pooh.

The point is that pigs are easily moved with a little boldness, a good board and some food. You can get them to go almost anywhere with a tasty apple or some pellets. It is also the only way to get them to return once they have made their bid for freedom.

Artificial Insemination

If you want to rear piglets you can either rent a boar, who should be able to do the rest with little trouble, or buy sperm in little vials to insert into the pig yourself. This is a complex matter that involves you being able to recognise oestrus, when the pig is fertile.

She will go off her food and at the same time her vulva will become reddened. Just as this starts to clear, you can get the pig to stand by pressing on her back, which shows she is completely ready to be impregnated.

Special catheters are used that are quite long, because it's a long way to the uterus. The pig starts rhythmic movements of muscles inside to move the sperm to the uterus and beyond. You insert the catheter until it will go no further and then twist it anticlockwise because the cervix has a screw top, as it were. Then the sperm vial can be added to the free end of the catheter, and finally introduced into the pig.

Gestation is three months, three weeks, three days (not three hours, three minutes and three seconds!) She will give birth to anything between three and a dozen piglets. You will know she is ready because she will start nest making. The sty, or wherever they are kept, will need heat from an infra red lamp and the pig will need a bar fixed a few inches from the ground to decrease the chance of her crushing them.

The mother will need extra feed, up to 25% more as she is producing lots of milk and plenty of water. Within hours she will be producing colostrum and then milk and all should go well. You should expect to lose some of the piglets. After about a month they should begin to forage for themselves and the mother should then start to have her feed ration reduced a little. Weaners can be sold at 8 weeks, which is probably how you got your first pigs!

Problems

There can be many problems with pigs. Keep them dry, well fed, well watered and stress free and most problems will be avoided. In an urban situation, dogs, cats and the flow of people can worry pigs, so try to keep them in the most secluded positions, but don't leave them alone for long periods. They like company and love a chat.

Get to know your animal – sickness is usually evident at both ends of the animal – feeding and poohing! If a pig is sick it will often get diarrhoea and go off its food. They are best if you can find fresh land for them to demolish. I knew someone who had pigs on five allotments and he simply moved them from one plot to the next every couple of months, snatching crops between them as he could. It was quite a complex rotation, but it worked for him.

If you cannot keep them off the same land pigs will need to be wormed regularly for gut and lung parasites.

Chapter Four

Urban Poultry

The popularity of poultry is increasing so much that you can buy them almost anywhere, including garden centres. After a long absence, pet shops are selling them again and even the odd hardware store. If you are buying poultry for the first time you should get together with people who know something about them, and the various poultry clubs can give you excellent advice. Find a local hen keeper and learn a lot from them first of all.

It could be said that the popularity of chickens these days is due to a number of things. Firstly, the television programmes where Hugh Fearnley-Whittingstall and others have highlighted the plight of battery and large flock farming birds have made people wonder about just where their eggs and meat come from. Then there is the way the trendy Eglu chicken houses have given the garden chicken run some style. Perhaps for the first time the keen gardener has a choice of materials that might be in keeping with the rest of the garden. There are now a large number of companies providing excellent traditional wooden poultry houses as well as the plastic systems.

Buff Orpington

White Plymouth

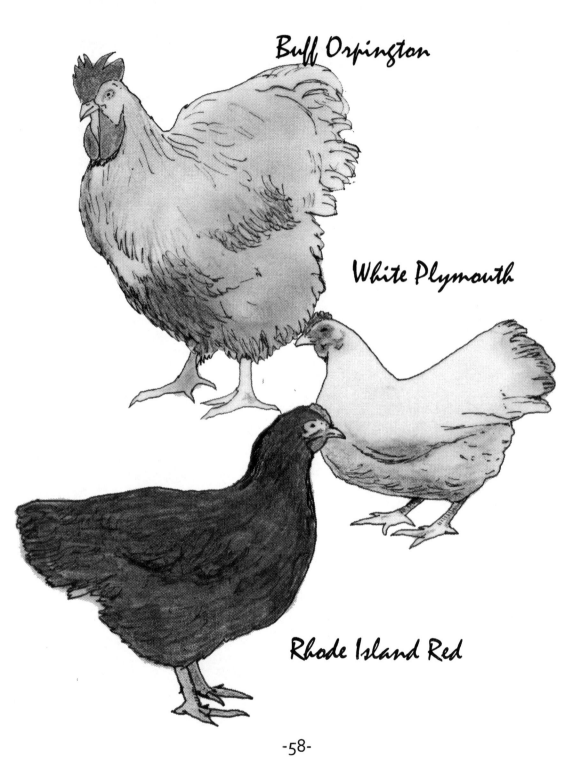

Rhode Island Red

They Make Great Pets

Chickens make fantastic pets. They are for the most part docile and keep themselves to themselves. Recently a little boy climbed into our neighbour's garden. They have had hens for a few weeks, just a couple of them. He went in to retrieve a ball while the hens were out wandering around. When he saw them he froze with fear and cried for help. He was frightened to death; I think he would rather have faced our dog than those hens, but all they did was to cluck and scratch at the grass.

It is a good idea to institute a regime of hand washing whenever children (or adults for that matter) collect eggs or arrange bedding and clean out the run or hut, but apart from this there are few problems.

Bantams, which are often more intelligent than the larger breeds, can be kept in the back yard. They are extremely easy to look after and are often great companions. They even make friends with humans and sometimes prefer the company of one over another.

The Economics of Eggs

In the spring and summer, as well as into the autumn, hens will convert whatever they find in the garden plus a handful of feed into two eggs every three days. Sometimes you will even get an egg every day for a few days. On average, depending on the breed, you will get between 180

Hens are nothing to be frightened of, especially if you choose not to have a cockerel. They will care for themselves on a day-to-day basis and not trouble anyone. They soon become used to human contact and animals kept in the garden are quite clean and disease free.

The Urban Farmer

Like any pet or animal there is always a lot to learn and you will never stop learning. But this is part of their charm. Poultry are certainly no more troublesome than keeping a dog; indeed for the most part they are easier because you don't have to be forever walking them.

and 240 eggs per bird each year. They will have consumed 365 handfuls of food costing two or three pence a feed. Your eggs will be costing you about half as much as the cheapest shop-bought eggs, but you have to take into consideration the cost of housing and other care such as wormers and feeders and whatever else you consider necessary. If you only have a couple of birds your savings will not be as great as if you had maybe six birds.

Needless to say, your eggs will be free range and your birds will not be filled with chemicals either. And there is all the difference between an egg bought in the supermarket and one just taken from the nest box and consumed the same day. No amount of money can buy that freshness – and there really is a difference in the quality between the home egg and the shop-bought one.

Better Lives for the Birds

Anyone who keeps poultry is doing hen kind a favour. By far the majority of poultry spend their lives in awful conditions, but we are not going to go into this subject – this isn't meant to be a guilt trip. However, the truth is that chickens able to see the light of day, that are cosseted and cared for and able to live in such a way as to be 'chicken normal,' have to be happier than caged birds or birds kept with thousands of others in a shed.

But that is the problem; the concept of happiness is somewhat blurred when you are a chicken. Some people think that a chicken in a cage is quite contented so long as it is warm and well fed with plenty of water – the optimum conditions to produce eggs. Some believe that chickens can't be 'happy' in the human sense, but I personally think that animals are somehow driven to care for themselves and when their bodies deteriorate because of their surroundings they simply cannot be happy in any sense, chicken or otherwise.

Children Love Them

Apart from the fact that a lot of children keep poultry for themselves there are a number of Poultry Club members under the age of 13, possibly because children simply love chickens. The whole package of poultry keeping, from collecting eggs to feeding to chick raising, even worming and cleaning out, is a wonderful way of communicating the wonder of nature to children. The number of schools keeping hens has increased considerably over the last year. There is something about caring for animals that brings out the best in children. Speaking as a former schoolteacher I cannot count the number of times even the very naughtiest of my children have been mesmerised by a chicken or a set of chicks in the classroom.

If you have young children, keeping hens is far better for them than any toy they might care to mention.

They are Easy

Keeping chickens is not beyond the wit of anyone. Only once have I seen a really bad case of neglect and this was with a man who became mentally ill, poor chap. He had hundreds of hens and had built fantastic sheds for them. His hens were wonderfully looked after until he became poorly. The problem was that no one noticed that he was ill and it was very unpleasant. But even at his worst he still managed to look after most of his birds reasonably well because they more or less looked after themselves.

They need somewhere to sleep that is safe and dry. It doesn't have to be all that warm. They need access to clean water and food and they need a little space to move around. They also love to scratch in the earth. The weaker ones would prefer a run that gave them a chance to stay out of the way of the stronger ones, but you rarely if ever see them fighting. Their food can be put in hoppers or fed individually every day and they need their sleeping quarters to be regularly cleaned. On the whole that's all it takes.

They're Cheap

Compared to almost any other animal or pet chickens are cheap. Perhaps not as cheap as a goldfish, though I won't tell you how much I spent at a fair once trying to win one of those. You can splash out and buy chickens with a really posh cover from Eglu and, although not the cheapest, these are very popular and exceptionally well designed. Then you can go to the garden centre and buy a hutch and a pair of birds for £100. It is important to buy birds from people who know about them. You will find all the advertisers in 'Home Farmer' actually know about their birds and will give you lots of help and support. There is nothing wrong with telling a reputable dealer that you are new to keeping poultry. You can even ask them who else they have sold to locally so that you can get some back-up.

Lots of Help

The Poultry Club of Great Britain at www.poultryclub.org is centred more on showing poultry in competitions, but has members all over the country who will be able to point you in the right direction to get help when you need it.

Many people look at their first chickens and wonder how they are going to stay alive! They worry about how much to feed them and if the security of their hut is enough to keep the foxes and other wildlife at bay. A five minute talk with an expert, usually the person selling them, is all you need to get you going with confidence. They will show you what and how to feed and how to do things like clip their wings to stop them flying over the fence into next door's garden.

Compost

Chickens are an ideal part of a good gardening system, especially for those who are looking to be more self-sufficient. A hen will produce a couple of kilos of droppings a month and this is ideal for turning into rich compost. It is said that hen manure makes the very best compost there is. If you use straw as bedding material, cleaning out the hutch provides you with a nutrient-rich material to be placed in the compost heap. It is really good if you can manage to compost the poultry bedding separately from the other garden waste. You can seed this composted material with mushrooms and get a great crop before putting it on the soil, where it is particularly good for brassicas of all kinds.

The ability to use the fertility of the chicken feed a second time is a great bonus and is a fundamental part of a balanced system of gardening.

Recycling

Chickens are brilliant for recycling. There is a great debate about the legality of giving them kitchen waste to eat, but most people do. But then you can use shredded newspapers in their bedding and ash from the fire or wood ash from the garden bonfire for them to dust bathe in. You can use eggshells in the garden for suppressing slugs and snails and to enrich the compost heap – there are so many ways of achieving frontline recycling using chickens.

Chickens in the Garden

It is possible that you are not allowed to keep poultry for the following reasons. Firstly they might be prohibited on the deeds to your property in which case there is little you can do about it, save by legal redress to the deeds, which is a difficult task and somewhat beyond the scope of this book.

Presumably your neighbours will be aware you are planning to keep poultry and this will conjure up all forms of horrific problems in their minds. Will there be rats? Will they be noisy? Will they fly over the fence and ruin my garden? Will we all die from Bird Flu?

It Is up to You to Win Them Over

First of all there needn't be rats, or any more rats than normal. Indeed it is people that attract rats more than chickens. There are many things you can do to keep rats away, and it's cheaper in the long run. Firstly you should keep your chicken feed well away from the chickens and only feed them a handful a day each – more or less. This will mean there is no waste for the rats to eat and no hoppers full of food for them to raid.

Secondly, keep the chicken hut completely clean at all times – this way there are no smells either. Collect the eggs daily and look out for signs of rats – holes being gnawed in the sides of buildings etc. For goodness sake don't leave rat poison down. If you compost material from the hut, make sure it is in a sealed container because rats can smell and they put two and two together.

Hens are quite noisy. Early in the morning they chirrup in a deep way, like smarties playing a clarinet (Don't ask!) but it is altogether a pleasant sound. Cockerels on the other hand are completely rowdy in a bullying way. But you do not need cockerels to keep hens. You will still get eggs whch will all be infertile.So you don'thave to keep a cockerel – these are not mammals! You will get just as many eggs out of hens with no cockerel present!

My first ever hens were kept on an allotment. It was spring and the plots were full of young cabbages. I put my new birds in the pen with a 2 metre fence around it. The following morning my birds were busily eating the young crops and my name was mud. It was then that I learned how to cut the feathers of one of their wings to keep them from gaining enough height to get over the fence.

Pleaxse note that there are also enough wild birds in the cities these days to get bird flu. Around 30 years ago I was involved in bringing the first Canada geese from Martin Mere to my local nature reserve. It cost £50 for a pair of birds. Now there are thousands of them! There are plenty of birds around to bring bird flu to our doors without any assistance from hen kind.

A Few of the More Popular Breeds

Rhode Island Red

These are a heavy, active breed. Bright and alert, they enjoy foraging on grass, make great pets and are relatively hardy. They will produce a large amount of brown eggs a year.

The Sussex

Originating not unsurprisingly in Sussex, these are dual purpose birds and one of the most productive breeds available. The hen will lay around 260 large eggs that are cream to light brown in colour. They are an alert but docile breed that can adapt easily to any surroundings. They are good foragers. Whilst they are quite happy to be free range, they will also be fine if kept in a confined space. They can occasionally go broody but this does not happen very often. The speckled is the most likely of the breed to do this.

Orpingtons

These birds love to be free range. They have a very strong tendency to go broody and therefore make great mothers. Their eggs are small and pinkish. They are greedy birds and need exercise to keep fit. Their wingspan is short so they can be kept in areas with low fences.

Plymouth Rock

These are friendly birds which are easy to tame. They are also vigorous and hardy and don't need a lot of space but do appreciate the chance to run free. They are not good fliers so do not require high fencing. They lay a good number of cream coloured eggs, averaging around 200 per year. Plymouth Rocks do tend towards broodiness though, so regular egg collecting is important to avoid too much of this. Chicks feather up quickly and make wonderful pets for children due to their docile nature.

Black Rock

A friendly docile bird and probably one of the most successful hybrids for modern free range. A highly developed natural immune system means they have the potential to have a long and productive life.

The Urban Farmer

Housing

Chickens need to be shut in overnight, or else the fox will get them – let alone some of the terrible cats and dogs that prowl the night gardens. The house can be either wooden – traditional – or plastic – such as the modern Eglu available these days. A lot of people used to traditional wooden houses complain about the plastic nature of the modern hen huts but they have one great thing in their favour. They are so chic that they are almost instantly acceptable to neighbours. It is design bringing the keeping of chickens in the garden once again into vogue – and not before time I say.

Chicken houses should have a roosting bar and a nesting box, and more importantly still, a really strong lockable door.

Feed

The best way of starting with poultry is probably with point of lay birds. These are about 22 weeks old. You can tell if a bird is ready for laying by gently thrusting two fingers into the gap in her pelvis, more or less up her bottom. If there is room for an egg to get through it is time for her to start laying.

These birds need to be fed on layers of pellets or mash, depending on which you prefer. Pellets have always been my preference because they are easier and neater to use. Along with this you can feed them any number of different extras, but the law requires that feed destined for humans should be separate from that destined for animals. You will get away with reasonably small amounts of feed from the kitchen scraps, but this should never, in my opinion, include any traces of meat at all – even gravy.

It is probably better to feed your hens from a trough or plate rather than allowing the feed to be scattered on the ground – and this is probably more important in the town than anywhere.

What Came First, the Chicken or the Egg?

The hen needs to go through many changes before she becomes a fertile, egg laying creature. The first cells that come, once the egg is fertilised, become all the eggs the bird will ever lay. So it is possible to say with some certainty that in embryological terms at least, the egg

Normally any hen has very little choice about the act of mating; romance is always a little rough in the poultry world. But when she is broody and has a clutch of eggs to sit on she is very much ignored by all the others.

To be honest, broodiness is a pain unless you want to increase your flock. If you use an incubator to bring your eggs on then you can really do without broody hens altogether. But you also then have to play mother.

always comes first!

John Seymour's method of raising young chickens was very natural. A broody hen would be allowed to take her offspring, and any others, off into the woods and they would return after a couple of months with young birds ready to join into the rough and tumble of poultry yard life.

Broodiness is more than a hen bird's urge to sit on hens. It controls her life for many months to come. Her behaviour becomes compulsive, repetitive and, above all, a little secretive. Her comb becomes less brightly red – probably a signal to everyone else, especially the males, to leave well alone.

Broodiness is partly controlled by an increase in the hormone, prolactin. This is in turn stimulated by prevailing light conditions and the availability of good quality nesting material and boxes. What passes for the pituitary gland in the chicken brain stimulates and controls many other hormonal processes. Some research suggests that the broody hen is stimulated by warm days and fresh hay. The whole cycle is initiated mentally and the rest of the process produces a number of hormonal changes that create both the behaviour and physiological changes.

This mental aspect to broodiness seems to explain why it can be catching in some flocks, particularly bantams that have a greater tendency towards broodiness.

For a start, a broody hen will go for long

periods without eating and drinking, and sometimes needs to be shifted off the eggs to force her to take water. Her underside feathers become more sparse and contact with her clutch is increased. This is called an incubation patch and again is controlled by hormones.

There are stages to broodiness, each one separated by a few days. Firstly the bird goes off her food and gathers eggs together for sitting, then sits and clucks. At the time of hatching the clucking increases which, together with the squeaks of the newly hatched chicks, encourages the hatching of the rest of the brood.

The hen's clucking takes several forms. Should you approach the sitting bird she will squawk loudly, warning you away. When she is content she chirrups and clucks in a soft low tone. The many variations of sounds coming from the mother hen are an important communication tool to be learned by the chicks – something that starts to happen before the animals come into this world.

The behaviour that started with sitting takes it out of a hen. They work very hard leading their chicks to safety, food and water in addition to the constant effort of sitting. But her ordeal continues for at least six weeks after the chicks are born.

The pecking order of a group of hens is by no means like that in human society. Young chicks are at the very bottom of the pile and are just as likely to be eaten by the other hens as by any other predator. The hen and her chicks need to be kept away from the rest of the flock and provided with shelter, chick food and water. The broody hen needs attention too. She will almost certainly be run down, be susceptible to parasite attack and should not be treated harshly.

Breaking a Broody

Stopping a broody hen from being broody is possible – you just have to take your time. There are a number of tricks you can use. The development of an incubation patch means the bird doesn't like being cold underneath. If you put her in a cage with a strong wire bottom, so that when she sits it is cold, then it will take a week, but she will eventually give up. Make sure that during this time the bird has access to food and water.

I knew a keeper who put the bird under a bucket for as long as it took without food and water and, whereas this worked every time, it is very harsh on the bird. I have read of people putting ice cubes under the bird after removing the eggs, but I haven't tried this myself.

The trick is to reverse the process that leads to a hormonal change. The bird doesn't give up being broody just as an act of will. It is the prevailing conditions which stimulate hormonal changes back towards normality. For the most part keeping the bird away from any other and making sure there is no inviting nesting material usually does the trick.

Incubation

There are many reasons why incubation is a good idea for increasing your stock. First of all you might not have a broody hen. It is also difficult for a hen to bring up a dozen chicks and there are losses to account for.

If you decide to incubate eggs you will have a problem. What are you going to do with the males? At some point you are going to have to kill them.

The incubator should be the best you can possibly afford. Cheap ones that hold only a dozen eggs could leave you with problems. You might get a hatch rate of 50% and thence only 2 hens (or worse) from the 12 eggs you bought.

Eggs remain fertile for up to three weeks and take 21 days (more or less) at 37.50°C to hatch. They need to be turned during this period so their membranes do not stick to the side of the shell. Unturned eggs will usually die.

When they start to pipe the eggs need to be removed from their supports in the incubator, leaving them flat on the floor. They will all hatch within a day of each other, though the last ones might have difficulties. It is best to try and leave them alone. Sometimes they are stuck to the shell or might have deformities and the best thing to do to them if they are not perfect is to kill them.

Keep them in the incubator for 24 hours and then in a box with a bulb for warmth. They should be fed chick crumbs and water should be available. Put pebbles in the water so the chicks cannot drown.

After a week move them to a more permanent position such as a run with high walls to deter rats etc. They still need heat and after 4 weeks should be put on a grower's ration. Keep them separate from the other birds in your flock until they are 18 weeks old. If you can put them in separate runs so they can see each other they will mingle more easily later. They are at point of lay (POL) at 22 weeks.

Keeping Ducks

Ducks have many sides to their character. They certainly are clowns who will make you smile. Grave and severe with each other, they are strong and courageous, yet timid and secretive. Keeping ducks is like keeping bees; they fascinate and you can watch them all day long and still be intrigued by their habits. They give the most fantastic eggs, with some breeds providing almost as many eggs as a hen.

You will read in some places that ducks do not need water but I believe this to be silly. The main problem is that they do not have good tear ducts so their eyes can get all messed up. They don't particularly need a lot of water, but it is better if they have access to flowing water rather than a bowl on the floor. They do like a good dunk in water in the morning, and will return several times during the day for a good splash.

Breeds of Duck

Most ducks are descended from the Mallard. Mallards are very prolific and interbreed easily. Their major point of recognition is the speculum, a flash of coloured feathers on the side. This is usually a bright, almost electric blue and is very noticeable. In modern breeds this has disappeared for the most part, but when you breed your own you may find it reappearing.

There are many duck varieties. Over the years people have bred them for either meat or egg production and produced a specification for the breed. The utility ducks you are more likely to have in the garden might not correspond to the actual breed specification, but this doesn't matter too much, so long as they lay, or grow, but probably more importantly, entertain.

Campbell

These were bred by a Mrs. Campbell and they are very productive egg layers. They can lay around 300 a year, as many as a good Marran hen. They are a typical shaped duck, by which I mean they don't stand up too much. Usually on the feed all day long, they are brilliant at finding slugs and insects.

Indian Runners

These come from the east, and it is thought that ships' captains brought them back from their travels and bred them in Scotland. If you see what appears to be a bottle of wine run across the garden it is most likely an Indian runner.

They are good layers, producing around 250–300 eggs and are a little smaller than the Campbell. They keep themselves apart in a mixed group and are extremely attractive.

Muscovy

The Muscovy is a breed of duck from South America entirely unrelated to the Mallard.

A really healthy duck, the Muscovy looks as though it is a small goose that has been messing around in the paint shed. They are genetically different from mallards, but you can interbreed them to produce a duck called a mallard mule. Muscovies are great for meat production but do not produce that many eggs. They really are fantastic to watch around the garden, although they can be a bit bossy, as a scar on the back of my leg will testify.

Aylesbury

I went to Aylesbury and looked everywhere for a duck, but couldn't find any. If you live there and have some I'd love to hear from you. Another large white breed, the ducks will produce around 120 eggs a year and put on a lot of weight. They seldom wander far from water and can be seen shuffling around looking for food.

Feeding

So long as the ducks have access to water, you can more or less treat them like chickens. They will grow merrily on layer's pellets plus green stuff and the run of the garden. They will do fine from three months old on layer's pellets, but they need to be on growers' pellets before that and up to a month old should be on chick mix. The birds should be fed around 100g a day at three months rising to around 300g a day at six months. By then they are at their adult weight.

Some birds, such as Aylesburys, guzzle as much food as they can, so feeding them daily rather than from a hopper is probably a good bet.

Housing

Ducks are not that bothered about the type of housing. Some roost, others don't. As long as there is plenty of straw and a safe lock to keep the fox away they are fine. They are not that good in direct sunlight, but can cope with extremes of cold very easily. Since they have waxier feathers, they cope with rain much better than hens.

Happy on grass, they chip away at plant edges and scour the ground for insects and slugs – they can get through a large number of slugs and prefer them to cabbages, so they are great on allotments. If you don't have grass to keep them on, you can use bark chippings for them to walk on, something frequently done with a couple of ducks in a run system.

You should change the chippings regularly, or move the birds to new grass as frequently as possible to avoid a build up of parasites and once a week you should change the bedding in their hut.

A few notes on geese

The best guard dog you'll get are a pair of geese, but you need a little space. You can feed geese almost entirely on grass if you have enough space. They prefer short grass. If you have no space for them, and a goose will need about a tenth of an acre, you should augment their feed with wheat. This can be fed on a tray with some water on top – they will take the feed through the water and rats wouldn't even know. They need about 200g of wheat a day.

Ducks and geese suffer quite badly from worms and so you will need to treat them as soon as you buy them.

For housing they only need a lockable shed to prevent them from being taken by foxes. They need a largish nest box too and they will lay frequently if you keep on taking the eggs away. If you leave the eggs the birds will begin to sit on them.

A few Notes on Turkeys

If you want to keep turkeys in an urban situation you will need understanding neighbours. This is because they make a lot of noise. You should consider keeping a trio of turkeys, frequently a male and two females, and for this you will need a 2m shed. They like to perch and will need plenty of space.

Turkeys are very hardy and generally easy to keep but, like most birds, they do not like wind or driving rain. They should not be kept with chickens for prolonged periods because they are more susceptible to blackhead than poultry and, although there are examples of the birds living well together, it's probably not worth the risk.

You should not consider feeding turkeys chicken layer's pellets because there is not enough protein in it. You can buy turkey feed from agricultural suppliers. Turkeys need fencing to keep them off other people's land and a good high fence is rather important. You can clip their wings – the outer flight feathers – but this gets progressively harder as the bird grows. If they are happy, content and well fed the simple presence of a fence provides a good impetus to stay put.

Killing turkeys isn't easy – they are strong birds and people resort to the broom handle method (used for geese too). However, the legality of this method is questionable, You are thus left with the stun bleed method, which is much better for the birds. Remember that you are not allowed to sell turkeys that have been killed by anyone other than a registered abattoir.

Keeping Quail

Quail are an interesting bird to keep and the eggs are delicately tasty.

There is something about quail that at first sight makes you think it is a bit of a waste of time. But this small bird can be very profitable for the smallholder who might be able to raise a few birds and sell the eggs at local hotels and restaurants and also in health shops and delicatessens.

You can find quail free and wild almost everywhere on the planet and increasingly on farms across the UK where they are not so wild and not so free. They convert feed to meat almost as efficiently as chicken and can be ready for the table in as little as five weeks. Moreover, they produce upwards of 240 eggs a year.

If anything, there is more yolk in a quail's egg. The major difference, apart from the size, is the nature of the shell and the inner membrane. They are tough little cookies, quail's eggs! You need to break into them with a heavy but sharp knife, but be careful; there is nothing worse than an egg with a broken yolk – whichever bottom laid it!

For the most part the nation's need for quail meat and eggs is met by a multitude of small farmers and smallholders and in the past has been fairly unprofitable. Upper Wood Farm near Ludlow was just such a venture where a few dozen birds were raised for local restaurants and delicatessens. The market was so meagre that even this tiny operation didn't last. Today, however, the market is much changed and quail meat can be found on supermarket shelves and their eggs can be purchased even in petrol stations.

Delicate

Food nowadays is often filled to excess with flavour. Frequently we try different foods in an attempt to be different. There is, however, a world of difference between flavour and taste. When a flavour hits you in the face you are expected to enjoy it. After all, it is a taste sensation! But we should, from time to time, enjoy the subtle and delicate. Certainly delicate does not imply bland. Quail's eggs are delicate. They are also creamier than a hen's egg and ideal for a kedgeree, boiled and sliced into two pieces and mixed with rice, peas and fish. Interestingly they are boiled for almost as long as larger eggs. A few seconds less than three minutes produces a yolk that is partly set but runny enough to make it interesting. Fried, they take only two minutes – but you can see what is happening in the pan anyway.

Keeping quail can be easy in that they are small. People might consider keeping them in small gardens just because they are small. But quail do pack a punch! They are the noisiest small birds when kept together in small spaces and they can fight like crazy. It is not unusual for birds to be very badly injured and sometimes shockingly so.

Young

Newly hatched quail are small and consequently have difficulty in keeping themselves warm. They need supplementary heat for at least three weeks and the temperature should be maintained at around 34°C. By a month old the birds are fully feathered and then start to become strongly territorial and whistle, a sound often refered to as piping.

They feed quite well on crushed chicken's laying ration and they need to be housed in a secure unit. I have used a large crate that has kept the birds predator free. There are also some examples of them living quite well with chickens.

Adding new birds to existing stock can prove difficult at best. Given their territorial nature it is probably a good idea to take the whole stock and mix them together in a completely new environment.

Poultry Problems

Everyone wants their birds to be in perfect health. Well that's what I thought until I got my first ever chickens. I inherited a run from a man on some allotments. There were dead bodies everywhere; rotting carcasses, skeletons and a complete mess in the hen house. Food was spilled everywhere and there was evidence of rats. It took a long time to sort out, I can tell you. But then, whenever the hens got sick, it was hard not to blame the previous occupant.

The problem is that hens do get sick and do so quite frequently! No matter how hard you try to keep things under control there is always something ready to come to the fore, so constant vigilance is important.

Good Health

It is important to be positive, so rather than start with what can go wrong, perhaps we should look at a healthy hen. Good birds should have bright eyes, a good even coloured and red comb, dry and clear nostrils, a bright full shiny coat of feathers with no real gaps – except during moult, plumpness and their bottoms should be clean.

Their behaviour should be alert and they should look 'perky' and alive, ever noticing things and quietly clucking away. They should be either feeding, scratching the earth, cleaning themselves, mating, avoiding mating but generally busy. Suspect any birds that stand in the same spot for a long time.

External Problems

If your birds have missing feathers this can be due to stress. Are there too many birds, are they bothered regularly by predators or children, are there enough perches, do you have enough nest boxes? Are there too many cockerels – especially if you have broken feathers on the hen's backs?

If you got some pristine hens and put them on completely pristine soil, with no problems at all, then pretty soon there will be problems with parasites. Goodness knows where they come from!

The poultry louse is flat and yellowish and is found where the hen is warmest – usually under the tail and around the bottom. They lay clusters of eggs at the feather base and they make the bird scratch. They are highly evolved and do not kill their hosts, but they are not pleasant for the animal.

I have never experienced the de-pluming louse – which does exactly what you would expect by irritating the bird so much it pulls its own feathers out. This is a summer-time problem. The feather mite, or the northern fowl mite, seems to be transferred by sparrows. They live all over the bird – especially at the bottom and in the neck. They will kill the bird eventually, and draw blood for food. They cause the bird to become listless and lose appetite.

All these mites and lice can be dealt with quite easily with a monthly dusting of lice powder. The same ingredients also come in spray form. Hold the bird firmly, preferably on its back, and rub the powder into all the nooks and crannies – especially around the bottom, under the tail, under the wings and on the neck. I wear rubber gloves and a mask to do this. These mites have a very short lifecycle, so they can get a hold quickly if you haven't treated your birds.

Dreaded Mites

All is going well. Your hens are living happily and laying normally until one day you notice their legs are not quite the same as they were. A bit scaly, a bit, well, rough looking. On closer inspection you cannot see anything, so you ignore it. Then you notice they are getting worse, and then, when you are changing the bedding in the hen house, you notice little mites like a rash covering the shady side of the perch. These red things, full of chicken's blood, move slowly away from the light like some crepuscular thing and for the first time you understand the natural world of farming.

Red mites have 8 legs and no body divisions, so they are arachnids, like spiders. They live off the animal during the day, hiding in crevices in huts, in nest boxes and anywhere they can find shade. During the night they march out, like a small army, onto the legs of the birds to pierce the skin and drink their blood.

Northern fowl mites stay on the birds all the time and so have a more devastating effect. You should look for listless or irritated birds. They will have a loss of condition, pale combs and wattles and you may find spots of blood on the eggs and the number of eggs produced will begin to drop. However, for red mites the easiest way of detecting infection is to look in the hen house where you will find them hiding from the sun.

Mites also carry other problems such as fowl cholera and, as the birds become more heavily infested, they cannot replace the lost blood quickly enough. This leads to anaemia and other immunological problems. They can then go down with almost anything.

Recognising northern fowl mite is a rotten task. You will find mites near the neck and around the vent, along with their eggs and faeces. The feathers are stained dark and I cannot stand them running onto my hand. (Yes! I know I'm squeamish!)

Treatment

The best treatment for red mite is to keep them down to absolute minimum levels by getting them where they spend the day. Clean out the hut and give it a jet wash as often as you can. If the hut is wooden, use a blowtorch around the crevices. Fill them in with putty and you can also buy products to treat the surfaces. Covering with sunflower oil slows their return. Make sure you get into the nest boxes. The mites can live for six months on a single belly full of blood, so you have to be on your metal!

You can also buy powders and sprays to treat the birds but it is virtually pointless treating them if you are not going to treat the hut. Pyrethroids, organophosphates, carbamates, citrus extracts, vegetable oil and mineral-based products (both liquids and dusts) have been used to control red mite in the environment. For northern fowl mite it is essential to apply approved insecticides to the affected birds.

If you do use chemical control methods, and for northern fowl mite there is little else available, you need to ensure that the birds are treated each fortnight and you have to ensure that the appropriate set aside periods areadhered to before the birds are killed for meat. There are lots of treatments available where the eggs have no set aside.

It is likely that you will not be able to completely remove these pests from your flock. Keeping them to an absolute minimum is important. Your control methods should include the provision of dust areas for the birds to treat themselves natuarally. Also make sure that the outside of the hut is disinfected, treated and clear of pests.

Red mite in particular will crawl deep into the wood, especially if it is old and rotting wood, and so may emerge again at a much later date.

Move Them Around

Internal parasites, or worms (though they are not all worms as such and have nothing to do with any earthworms your hens might scratch up out of the ground) build up in the land the hens are on, so it is a good idea to move your birds from one pasture to the next to give the land a rest if possible.

There is much to be said for keeping hens healthy and happy – because in this way their own immunity deals with most of the worm problems. Most internal parasites of poultry are based in the gut and so are not passed on to humans.

Other infestations or stress can affect the hen's immunity and cause them to become more susceptible to internal parasites. On the whole you can treat a flock by adding worming powder, which is a special preparation available from feed stores, to the hens' feed. You can spot a bird that needs worming by its listlessness; it will be frequently off its food, will stand still and shiver and seem to stare into space.

I have not used natural remedies for worming birds such as strong garlic preparations etc, because I don't fancy the idea of garlic flavoured eggs. On the whole they have been kept under wraps by good flock management

Coccidiosis is a very common and costly problem in poultry. This unpleasant disease can cause all sorts of painful symptoms in both young and old birds.

Coccidia live everywhere; in the soil, in the guts of most animals but are mostly found in faeces. It is almost certain that this single celled parasite will be present somewhere in the soil that your birds are scratching and feeding on. When the conditions are not perfect the cells create microscopic egg-like cysts which can remain dormant in the soil. These are then ingested by the birds causing them to become infected.

These cysts, knows as oocysts, can last for a year and are resistant to drying out, freezing cold and a number of disinfectants. Once inside the bird they find a niche in the specific part of the gut the particular species prefers. There are seven species that infect poultry and they are all quite specific in their requirements. Some birds have a degree of built in immunity and symptoms can vary according to the amount of infection.

Symptoms come and go according to the coccydial load (the number of parasites in the gut) and other external factors that can range from cold weather, other infestations, social pressure, feeding and so on. In particular, the free availability of vitamins A and K in feed have an effect in keeping coccidian concentrations down. Flare up can be very sudden and you should be keen to recognise any changes in your birds' health.

In particular rescue poultry can fall prey to coccidiosis should they be forced into an environment of high soil load and a lot of 'natural' or untreated food that they can find difficult to eat after their life-long incarceration in a cage eating easy swallow food.

The protozoan parasites inter-set themselves between the cells of the gut and this causes a number of problems. First of all it makes the animal feel unwell, leading to a loss of appetite. The reduction in the capacity of the gut causes other problems too. It becomes harder for the bird to absorb the nutrients it needs and when the coccidian cells have passed a threshold number the gut wall begins to break down. This causes diarrhoea and, within days, blood will be seen in the watery droppings.

The problem affects mainly young birds that are subject to high loads and low anti-coccidiant feed concentrations. They have not usually had the chance to develop any immunity and, as their guts are not fully vaccinated from food sources, are still in the early stage of development. In these cases the parasite load increases without check.

Lethargy, muscle waste and a general lack of condition is common in birds that have had a prolonged and gradually increasing exposure to the parasite. Internally this affects the ability of the animal to maintain its immune system and various other problems can be seen in conjunction.

They can fall to other diseases, especially respiratory ones, and can suffer very badly from red mite attack. Their combs become pallid and lack colour and their overall appearance deteriorates. A heavy infestation will have the bird looking as though it is near death – wings drooping, eyes closed and feathers ruffled. The sudden death of birds is frequently down to coccidiosis, particularly in the case of rescue birds and young.

Infestation can predispose the animal to other intestinal diseases, especially necrotic enteritis (NE). This is caused by the bacterium clostridium perfringens, a soil-born organism that is found almost everywhere. When it grows unchecked in the gut, it releases toxins that damage the intestinal lining.

Good Management

Your management skills will actually help your birds gain a measure of immunity and will keep the coccidial population to a minimum. While the parasites are in the spore stage they can easily be removed. Dryness enhances this, forcing the coccidian into the spore stage. If there is nothing in the hen house that is wet, nor appetising in terms of pecking, the likelihood of the birds ingesting large amounts of infected faeces is lowered. Keep the bedding dry.

From the hen house a few yards into the run, a series of duck boards, or even wire netting for the birds to walk on will also keep the chance of ingesting infected material to a minimum. Clearly, the more birds you have the greater the chance of infection. Overcrowding is one of the main contributing factors. Needless to say, this disease costs the poultry industry over £40 million a year.

Investigations of broiler sheds have shown that the oocysts will remain viable for over a year where they are protected from prolonged exposure to the weather. It is possible for the parasite to be transmitted into clean sheds by humans carrying the infection on clothing and boots. Introducing young birds into such environments will lead to inevitable infection. But the same is true for home, urban bird populations too.

The further away from the hut the less chance there is of the soil borne spores causing a problem, but good cleanliness, fresh soil, plenty of varied food and good ventilation all help keep the problem at bay. However, it is not recommended that you simply rely on your good works to keep the problem out of your flock.

What to look for

- Listlessness
- Off its food
- Lacking vigour
- Pale comb
- Ruffled feathers
- Blood in diarrhoea
- Open drooping wings
- Eyes closed

A Quick Guide to Parasitic Diseases

This is by no means intended as an exhaustive list, but it will serve as an effective guidif your birds are poorly. Please do not rely on this list as a definitive guide for diagnostic purposes as it is not meant to serve as such.

Intestinal Roundworms	Birds are droopy and have diarrhoea – worms visible
Cecal Worms	Can infect the bird with blackhead
Thread Worms	Mucosa become thickened, intestines destroyed, frequent death
Tapeworms	Slow growth, listless, low egg production, occasionally visible
Gapeworms	Found in the trachea, grunting (gapes) open mouthed breathing

Killing Chickens

People kill chickens all the time, by all sorts of methods. There are only two completely safe and 100% legal ways of doing it. A free bullet (a high powered airgun pellet will do) into the brain from a close distance followed by immediate bleeding, or electrical (or percussive) stunning followed by immediate bleeding. However, neck dislocation is also allowed, or at least tolerated, in cases where single animals are being killed. If you are killing chickens for sale or cooking them for the buying public, the correct certification is needed for both the killer and the premises and this will invariably include having used the correct stunning equipment.

Why is dislocation not recommended?

You have to be very skilled to ensure that the job breaks the spinal chord completely and thus kills the bird. Also the time taken for the animal to die is often quite considerable and there are numerous examples where the plucking has begun while the bird was still alive. For this reason Compassion in World Farming does not believe the procedure should be recommended. They advise that such animals should be bled after the initial signs of death have taken place.

It might be argued, and may well become law at some point in the future, that a time of two minutes for a beast to die represents an unacceptable period. Some are now saying that this time period means the "duty of ensuring an animal does not suffer distress or pain" cannot possibly be observed in such cases.

Why is using an axe not recommended?

You cannot be sure that in all cases a single stroke will sever the neck and death might require yet another another blow – or even a third! Most of the equipment required to cut the throat of the bird has to be sharp by definition, but you do not always find sufficiently sharp axes used for the job.

A bird with a damaged neck can take a surprisingly long time to die, although it has to be said that death from the severing of the head can appear to be instant, but it may take as long as 30 seconds for the bird's brain inside the head to die from lack of blood.

I would like to say from the outset that anyone who keeps poultry for their own food is doing bird kind a good service. It is not possible to compare the life of a well cared for bird in a garden to that of a bird in a broiler house!

How to kill by dislocation

Before killing, handle your birds regularly so it is no surprise to them that you pick them up and hold their legs. Separate the animal and deny it food for 24 hours, but give it plenty of access to water.

Collect your chicken gently and calmly and in one hand hold both legs in a firm grip. The head should be held in the other hand between the middle fingers so that the back of the head rests in the palm of the hand. Push down on the head end and twist. You will feel the bones break and the animal will begin to flap violently. Within 30 seconds the flapping will stop and the bird will be dead.

Hold or hang the bird upside down for the blood to fill the void in the neck, or cut through the neck to allow the blood to escape.

The same method is used for killing ducks, only you have to work harder because the animal is a good deal stronger. Geese and turkeys should be killed by stun and bleed unless you are an all-in-wrestler or a prop forward! The use of a stick to hold the head on the floor is not recommended by Compassion in World Farming because it increases the birds' distress.

How to kill by bleeding - The stun

You must use a stunning method that is seen to work properly. Take it as read that the free bullet is only another way of stunning the bird. You can buy hand held electrical stunning equipment or percussion stunning equipment. Consequently you will have to read the instructions on the model you use and make sure that you can use the equipment properly before you actually use it for its intended purpose.

Normally the bolt of a percussive stunner is matched to the type of bird and you need to make sure you use the correct charge for the beast. A poultry stunner is not guaranteed to work on a larger animal, so be sure what you are buying and use the correct equipment for the job.

The bleeding of the animal should take place within a few seconds of the stun and the whole operation should be swift.

Is It Dead?

The bird is dead when the convulsions cease and the eyes close. A good stun, particularly a percussive stun, usually kills the animal outright and it will convulse. If the bird continues to breathe rhythmically it is stunned, but there is no time to wait to inspect it, you know it is not all right. If you miss-stun you will know about it and so will the bird. You should kill the animal right away by neck dislocation.

Once stunned properly slit its throat. You should wait two minutes before starting to pluck the feathers, which you should do with sharp pulls against the grain starting with the flight feathers. Some people dip the bird in hot water at around 60°C for a minute and then pluck it wet. This can help, especially with bigger birds.

Chapter Five

The Urban Sheep

Sheep have a reputation for falling down dead, of giving up and of being stupid. Anyone who has read Far from the Madding Crowd will know that Gabriel Oak lost his flock off a cliff and many of them nearly died from getting into the clover field. They are not easily kept in an urban situation because they need grass, and dry grass at that, and in the city any green is all too often used for burning cars and walking the dog or worse. But it is possible to keep sheep these days in a number of important situations.

Firstly, if you have two acres of well fenced land you can keep as many as ten sheep and one of them can be a ram. You would need to be sure that the locals could not get to them and that their dogs are kept well away.

This illustrates a problem. You would be making, in farming terms, very little money from a dozen sheep and their offspring and you would always be eating mutton – but there is nothing wrong with that. The financial value of the land in urban terms would be much higher than the amount of money it was making. Of course, no one can stop you from doing what you want with your own land, but

Dorset Down

Kerry Hill

Ryeland

don't expect any financial assistance to do it.

Also, green space in an urban setting is a cause of great envy and you can guarantee that someone somewhere will want to build on it.

But today's sheep farmers are not making any money and many are going out of business. Sheep are disappearing from hillsides all over the country and this might just present a possibility. What would be the problem with the urban farmer buying sheep directly from the farmer at market prices while they are alive and running around the hillside? One could then tag along and learn about sheep first hand, do some of the duties of shepherding, shearing, drenching, foot care, treating for strike and, of course, lend a hand at lambing time.

Breeds

The UK boasts more sheep breeds than any other nation and there is practically a breed to suit every different environment: hill and dale, wet and dry, lush grassland to sparse vegetation.

Dorset Down

This is a popular breed for smallholders renowned for its docile, easy to manage character. The ewes make wonderful mothers and they produce active lambs at birth.

You could keep a couple of sheep as pets on a little less than half an acre and then take them to be tupped by a nearby farmer. Of course, before you even start, you will need a holding number and the sheep will have to be tagged and movements logged etc. You cannot simply keep sheep in the garden.

Ryeland

A dual purpose down (bred to live on grassland rather than hill) breed producing quality wool and a good carcase. There are white and coloured strains and they are docile and quite small, so they are relatively easy to handle. They don't have the natural escape tendancies of some of the primitive or hill breeds.

The Soay

The Soay has been used successfully in the reclamation of low fertility grazing; its light tread and ability to survive on sparse vegetation make it ideal for such work. The Soay ewe is an excellent mother, and Soay mutton has an excellent taste. They seek shelter more readily than other breeds of sheep due to their small body size and lightweight fleece.

The Jacob

This breed has high lambing percentages and they are easy lambers - essential for the novice or first-time sheep breeder. Jacob ewes show consistently good mothering qualities and many will give sufficient milk to rear triplets without recourse to bottle feeding. They have few disease problems and are relatively free of foot rot.

Feeding

Sheep nibble grass that cattle have pulled at. In other words they clean up after cattle and this makes them good in the winter on grass left by the cattle who are now indoors. They can eat the grass of about two large allotments, but you'd need much more space than this even though the stocking rate is the same. You can get about five sheep per acre, but they're not all eating evenly and the grass has to recover. In the winter the grass doesn't recover, so they will need extra food. They munch their way through about a kilo of barley and oats a day.

In lowland areas sheep are traditionally put into a field of mangel wurzels, beet or turnips and they do very well on this in the cold weather. They will eat up to 8kg of roots a day. In some areas you can still see the golden hoof method of putting sheep on winter wheat. They nibble the young grass like shoots and encourage branching. At the same time they dung the field and the wheat grows even more quickly because of their presence.

It is possible to keep sheep indoors in the winter and feed them hay and roots. They will need 2kg of good hay a day each with around 4-5kg of roots. So one regime would be to keep your sheep on grass just after lambing until tupping in early autumn. Then keep them indoors to include lambing, giving your meagre grass some respite and clearing the parasites.

Shearing

If you are keeping sheep for wool then the best regime for a small flock is to eat the two year olds after shearing and keep the new females as replacements. If you only have a few sheep, get them to your nearest neighbour and do the job with them. This is by far the best way to learn the job and is also the most cost effective..

The basic idea is to get the sheep in a comfortable position (for you) and clip the belly first up to the neck on either side. Then to cut in long swathes on either side until you reach the top of the back. Clearly this is a skill you have to learn first hand, so you need to get out there and find someone who can show you. There are plenty of courses at the various agricultural colleges.

Tupping

All this depends on how many sheep you have. It takes place in the autumn and you will need a good ram. You should decide what you are going to do with your sheep at this time. Normally you will have details of the birth records of your animals and should keep those which have had twins. Triplets can, however, be more trouble for the urban farmer than for conventional sheep farmers because they might need special attention which is not available. It might be difficult for a rejected lamb to be cared for in the home, for example. No one wants to be accused of cruelty – the usual lot of urban farmers doing normal farming activities. Lambs can bleat all night long and they sound not unlike children.

The ram is normally saddled with a bib that allows the sheep he has visited to be marked and then gestation begins, a process of 147 days.

Lambing

When your sheep are lambing, but certainly if it is your first time, get someone that knows what he is doing to help you. It might cost you a bit, but what value is education?

At around 120 days feed the sheep less roots and allow them to thin out a little or they will have problems in labour. Normally they see to the job themselves, but you have to watch them like a hawk. If she is straining for an hour or so you might need to get in there and help out.

You will need clean hands and a moveable pen is a good idea to constrain her movements. The most common problems are tiredness or the head of the lamb being in the wrong position. The first thing to look for is a pair of forefeet just protruding from the vagina. They will be wet and not at all easy to pull on, so tie them together with a soft chord such as an old tie and pull slightly downwards when she strains. Nine times out of ten this is enough.

If nothing happens don't use excessive force, but simply insert your fingers to find the head. It could be turned slightly upwards and thus forming a lock when the sheep strains. This is easily rectified by pushing the lamb back in and resetting the head position. Let the sheep strain again and the lamb will likely as not fall out.

Sheep suffer from many diseases but the major one is where the sheep effectively poohs on itself, attracting the attention of blowflies. They lay eggs in the pooh and the maggots then eat through its bottom! Sheep die from this and you can dip them in an insecticide to deal with it – but it is also cleared if you keep the sheep clean and cut the wool from around its bottom.

They do get fluke and other intestinal and lung parasites and there is nothing other than to treat them for worms. If you have only wet grassland consider draining it. This will considerably improve the health of your flock. Finally, especially for sheep on wet grass and indoors, their feet do need treating otherwise the horn will rot. You can simply cut the hard horn with pincers.

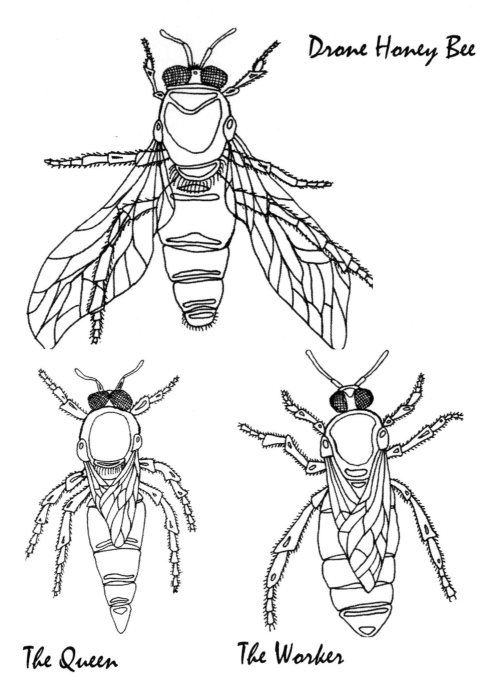

Drone Honey Bee

The Queen

The Worker

Chapter Six

The Urban Bee

Every urban farm should have at least one beehive. Indeed, every garden should have a beehive! Beekeeping has so many advantages that you should overcome your quite natural abhorrence to being stung, although there are also many natural advantages to being stung.

Beekeeping is essential to our continued existence as a species. Without them our crops would not be pollinated and without this there would be precious little food. But if I were to tell you that bees don't pollinate flowers haphazardly, they actually do it in an intelligent way to ensure the best results for themselves and for the crops too, you would be amazed. It is a well known fact that keeping a beehive increases the yield of pollinated crops by around 30%. That means that the fruit of your labours will be more plentiful just because you keep bees!

On top of this you get all sorts of products, some less obvious than you might have first imagined. Clearly everyone knows you get honey. This is obvious but what is less well known is that in a good season you can get around 60lbs of honey per hive. If you

The Urban Farmer

Time

A hive needs an hour's work a week with a little more at harvest time and a little less in the winter. You will also spend an evening at the beekeeping club learning the ropes. Bees are calming – there is no better way of overcoming the rush of the modern world and you will find yourself increasingly drawn to the apiary, just to watch the bees leaving and joining the hive.

never use sugar again it is clear to see that a couple of hives will keep the average family in sweetness for pretty much the whole year.

But it is more than just sweetness. Honey contains some pollen and this is collected from all the plants in your area. Now in the height of the summer I do suffer from hay fever caused by an allergic reaction to pollen and by taking honey with pollen in it I get an inoculation which gives my immune system a chance to get used to the onslaught before the summer comes. It doesn't completely cure the problem, but it does help enormously.

Wax is another important substance you get from beekeeping, but the modern way of keeping bees is expensive when it comes to wax and it is pretty difficult to harvest enough if you have to make frames year on year. A less modern approach, but one that is becoming more popular, is the top bar hive where the bees are kept in a box with what amounts to a stick of wood from which they draw out their own comb. This provides a greater opportunity for harvesting wax. Wax is useful for more than just candles. You can make all kinds of polishes, skin treatments, salves and balms from it too.

Propolis is gathered from the plant world and used by bees to perform a number of functions. Firstly, it is used to glue up the hive. They glue almost everything down. Secondly, it is used as an antiseptic. They encase animals that have died in the hive stopping them from rotting and thus infecting the hive. Propolis has remarkable properties, not the least being as a wonderful antiseptic.

Back to Stings

The scientific name for the honeybee is Apis, which is translated as 'healer' and even though there are many stings in a hive, beekeepers frequently live long and healthy lives. It is thought that bee venom has some curative action against arthritis. It is statistically true that arthritis is less prevalent in old beekeepers

Are Bees for You?

The following are the prerequisites for keeping bees of your own. You do not have to have your own bees to start with. The numerous beekeeping associations have lots of hives for you to learn on and this should be your first call in introducing yourself to the hobby.

Skills

You need a cool head, an eye for detail and a willingness to learn. Almost invariably you will find beekeepers to be a humble lot and both approachable and understanding. This is because the bee's way of life rubs off on the beekeeper. I have never found a group of people anywhere with a better understanding of the fact that 'everyone has to start learning somewhere.' Don't think that just because you don't understand the hive you cannot keep bees. If you can carry a box you can

When a worker bee is in distress it gives out an alarm pheromone which will be ignored by most of the bees, but if more bees are injured the alarm increases. This will have the effect of making the other bees more prone to attack in ones or twos and you will notice bees flying straight at the visor of your suit. This is often a warning. Remain calm and try not to breathe too heavily because your breath will excite them more.

have a beehive.

Equipment

The initial prerequisites are a bee suit, or at least a veil to protect your face, some beekeeping gauntlets or gardening gloves, a hive tool and a smoker.

Secondary equipment ranges from a good set of elastic bands to keep your clothes tucked in and keep the bees out, a bee brush or a feather for removing bees from your bee suit and a good bucket to store the bits of waste from your hive inspection.

A confession

I hate bee stings so I cover up. I wear a woolly under my beesuit and a pair of gloves under my gauntlets and a pair of rubber gloves on top. Sometimes I wear a cap under the hood to keep them from stinging my head. I look like an idiot, I get hot and other people call me a softie. I don't care! I just ask them if they would like to play rugby against me and get on with inspecting my hives!

Don't let fear stop you from keeping bees!

Space

A beehive is small and fits easily into a garden. You do need somewhere to put your equipment though. For every hive you have you will need another spare – just in case you have a swarm or need to repair something. In all you will need a corner of a shed for every hive.

You will also need to become a member of a local beekeeping society – this gives you some insurance and a whole load of help. So if the above has not scared you to death, beekeeping is for you!

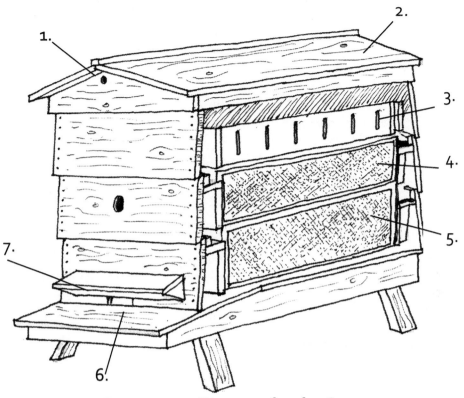

1. Bee escape, 2. Waterproof roof, 3, Super,
4. Honey frames, 5. Brood chamber, 6. Alighting board,
7. Entrance

Buying Bees

Bees are not cheap. Before the bee diseases of the last few years you could have expected to pay £50 for a colony, yet recently I have heard reports of them selling for five times this sum. You need to get bees from a colony that is free from disease otherwise you are just wasting your time. By far the best way of getting hold of bees is from your local beekeeping association.

Bees come in a box called a nucleus. Inside you will find four frames of bees, honey, eggs, developing grubs and a queen. The queen is usually colour coded so you can work out how old she is and some people clip the wings of the queen to stop her flying off in a swarm.

The Urban Farmer

The workers wear themselves out. (I know that feeling!) They travel many miles in their hunt for honey, work every hour of daylight of the 22 days of their foraging and usually succumb to exhaustion somewhere away from the hive. Any that die overnight in the hive are thrown outside by workers the following morning.

The frames are simply placed in their new home, the brood box of your hive. A brood box has room for between ten to twelve frames depending on the make and you introduce the nucleus frames to the centre of the box. The worker bees will quickly 'draw out' the blank frames to make honeycomb and the queen will lay eggs in them. Twenty two days later your new eggs will emerge and the numbers of bees will build up.

The first thing you need to do for your bees is feed them with sugar syrup – a mixture of equal parts of sugar and water and you will find all kinds of recipes as the months go by.

Inside the colony

The castes of the bee are often described as being Queen, Worker and Drone. However, this gives an incorrect emphasis. We often think that the queen is the most important bee in the hive, but this is not strictly accurate. So appropriately we shall start with the boss bee:

The Worker

Depending on the time of the year there are between a thousand and thirty thousand workers in the hive. The life of a worker bee is made up of three sections of 22 days. It spends 22 days developing as an egg and a grub, 22 days working inside the hive and then she wears herself out flying around collecting nectar and pollen for the final 22 days. The only workers to deviate from this are the ones that 'overwinter' in the hive.

Once they emerge from their cells they learn the layout of the hive and then start their housekeeping duties. Their days are spent feeding the queen, cleaning cells, feeding grubs, cooling the hive, cleaning the hive, evaporating honey, making repairs, protecting the hive, gluing things up (they love to do this!) and learning the language of bees.

At around 22 days they start to fly. First they take an image of the hive and its geography. Once they understand this they make longer and longer flights and start collecting nectar and pollen. Honey bees are complete masters at pollinating plants and your crops will be much improved if you have a beehive nearby.

Bee Decision Making

Many people have heard about the waggle dance, the way bees communicate the direction and position of a good food supply. But they are more interesting still. When a number of bees return to the hive from two competing food sources, the workers decide which one is best to exploit first. Once this one is exhausted, the other is started on.

Some worker behaviour is dominated by the queen, who keeps her place in the hive by emitting hormones. The workers know her peculiar cocktail of chemicals and will attack any intruders that do not smell of her. For this reason amalgamating queen-less workers with a queened colony needs to be done slowly so that the additional bees can accumulate their new queen's smell.

However, if the queen is not able to lay eggs properly, perhaps because of injury, the workers will force new virgin queen cells and kill the injured queen by clustering round her and literally cooking her – she dies from heat exhaustion.

The Queen

Her majesty is far from bossing the hive. She is simply an egg-laying machine. If she dies the workers will rear a new queen and if this fails the workers themselves will lay eggs. However, if this happens the colony is indeed on its last legs. (A queen-less colony is normally a very angry and noisy colony.)

The queen's job is to lay eggs and she will do so at an amazing rate, so long as there are clean cells to lay in and the temperature is high enough. She will lay fertilized eggs in ordinary cells and these will become workers. All the workers in the hive are sisters. She will lay unfertilized eggs in slightly larger cells made by the workers specifically for the purpose of raising males.

She will lay in a queen cell which is noticeable by the fact that it hangs from the bottom of a frame, or sticks out from the side of a honeycomb. This egg will be fed on a special substance, royal jelly, and this will cause the grub to develop into another queen.

Around May time the hive will naturally divide – something that beekeepers hate which is called swarming. Often the old queen, who gets out of the way of a newcomer, causes the swarm. Usually a queen is good for around three year's worth of eggs, except that by the beginning of year 3 her egg supply is significantly reduced. You can almost guarantee that a three-year-old queen will be near her last days.

Drones

These are male bees. They are larger than workers but smaller than the queen. They have only one function, but it is a very important one. They provide two things for the colony. Firstly, they provide sperm to provide the queen with the ability to create new bees. Secondly, they provide something given to them by their mother. This is genetic variation. When the queen produces drone eggs they are genetically slightly different to each other. This is the driving force of bee evolution, because at the end of the day the only hope bees have to overcome microbial advances against them is to be genetically diverse.

Drones fly with queens to pre-determined sites known to an antiquity of bees. The queen knows where this is and will fly to where there are many drones, unseen above our heads at some considerable height. The queen will mate with ten or more drones and collect a large amount of sperm that will last her for the rest of her life. Inside the queen are many billions of sperms, all genetically different and from many different drones – so it can accurately be said that the worker bees in a colony are only half sisters.

It is the workers that decide how many drones are provided for in the colony at any one time. The queen will only lay a drone egg in a drone cell and it is the workers who limit the numbers of drone cells in the hive. The queen herself has no say in the matter.

When the autumn comes the bees are in decline and the colony prepares for winter. Since it takes a teaspoon of honey to keep a honeybee going through the winter, the number of bees in the hive is drastically reduced. The drones are expelled from the hive and die outside of cold and hunger. The workers will not let them in no matter how desperately they fly around the entrance. Since drones have no sting they are powerless to resist. Many an interesting hour can be spent watching the workers expel drones again and again with increasing ferocity. The entrance to a November hive is littered with dead bodies.

Among the first eggs to be laid in the spring are the drones. They are needed to fertilise a a new queen, if one is necessary. She will need plenty of fertilized eggs as soon as possible if the colony has a hope of increasing its numbers in time to take advantage of the new nectar flow.

Looking in the hive can be a daunting thing to do for the first time

The problem with doing things for the first time on your own is that you forget. You spend all day worrying about what to do and in what order to do it and then it goes completely out of your head! When you are at the beekeeping club, with lots of people around you, it is very easy to be all macho and not worry about bees flying at you and crawling over your hands, but when you do if for yourself it's another matter!

It is completely easy to be freaked out by the bees coming at you a dozen at a time and nearly choking yourself on smoke fumes as you wildly puff away at everything!

The Urban Farmer

The easiest way to collect honey from the combs is simply to cut through the cappings and let the frame drain over a large bowl. This way you get some wax in the honey, but it doesn't really matter. Some people eat the comb with the honey in it anyway.

Relax!

Your first dip into the hive should be a short one. Get into the habit of only spending the minimal amount of time in the hive anyway, it's best for the bees.

Spend ages getting the smoker working. I'll let you into a secret, never to be repeated! My first time I 'went solo' I couldn't get the smoker to light. So I poured a tablespoon of meths in it and still it wouldn't work, so I took a blowlamp to it. It went up like a rocket and I burned the veil of my bee suit and couldn't go into the hive anyway! The answer is to take your time!

Flyers

The first thing to look for is flying bees. They should, assuming it is summertime and a good warm day, be flying out of the hive and returning as though you were standing by a bee motorway. They should be coming in and out with purpose and aiming for the entrance of the hive. Have a look for any bees that might be squirting near the hive, which would indicate an illness such as nosema. Then look into the entrance to see if there are any bees fanning, which would indicate that they are too hot.

Make sure the water supply is clean and full – which might be a saucer. I always put some clean gravel on the saucer to prevent the bees from drowning.

Finally, inspect the outside of the hive for any damage from woodpeckers, dogs, badgers, thrown bricks and the like.

Stand Aside!

The first thing to do on going into the hive is to stand away from the entrance. In the five minutes you are in the boxes you can get covered with a lot of bees, each trying to get inside and it is a real pain trying to get them off your back when you are on your own. Position yourself at the side of the hive and give a little puff of smoke at the entrance. This is a warning to the bees that there is fire nearby.

Remove the lid and any crown board you might have and give a little puff of smoke over the bees that you can see.

The idea is not to incinerate them with a flame thrower; a gentle waft of good thick smoke is all you need. If you burn them they will die, or become very mad. Frankly, I'd prefer them dead rather than mad!

As you waft them with smoke they will move down into the spaces between the frames and fill up with honey. This makes them less likely to sting. But from now on the bees that fly at you will mean business. To cut down the chances of being stung, avoid both perfume and bad breath. They also don't like beer, so have a pint afterwards!

Also, cover up! A hat under my veil helps to keep the mesh off my face. The number of times I have been stung on the chin!

Easing Out

Use the hive tool to unstick the supers and the queen excluder. Don't simply lift the super, but lift and twist it a little on the way up. Stand the super on the hive lid and inspect the queen excluder. You are looking for the queen just in case she is walking on the underside. If she is there gently shake her off onto the brood frames. Place the queen excluder on top of the supers. This will tend to keep whatever bees are in there all in one place.

Use your hive tool to ease out the brood frames. You are looking for the queen and if you cannot find her then you are looking for eggs in cells or grubs in cells. The frames should have a good few hundred

The Urban Farmer

bees on them and you can shake them off into the box.

As you go along the hive, scrape off all the bits of comb the bees have used to glue it up, keeping the wax of course! You are also looking for queen cells

Why Look in the Hive at all?

You should avoid going into the hive every day or so. Bees are not pets and if you examine them too frequently you will lose them. In the spring you will check them less frequently than in the early summer, mostly because of the weather. Of course in the winter they should be left well alone. You should only enter the hive when the temperature is above 15°C, when it is not raining heavily and the wind is no more than light.

Inspection will normally give an indication of the colony strength, how much food they have or might need and the health of the queen. You will be able to judge if you need to take any remedial action, add a super, give some food, remove queen cells, requeen and so on. Of course, you will also be able to check the colony for signs of disease.

Approaching the Hive

Make sure your smoker is properly lit and delivering good quantities of smoke. Do not stand in front of the bee's entrance and give a little puff of smoke into the hive from below before you remove the lid. This gives the bees forewarning of fire and they will start to take honey. The honey makes them more rotund and less liable to sting, though this is by no means guaranteed.

Remove the lid and place it upside down to the side of the hive. You will stack your other components on top of this, save perhaps your crown board and queen excluder, which you might lay against the side of the hive.

Apply another puff of smoke underneath the crown board as you lift it.

Do not pump the smoker as though it were a steam train: it will get increasingly hot and your fuel will burn too quickly. Give a couple of short puffs away from the bees to make sure it is still lit and then smoke the bees with a single waft with a simultaneous squeeze of the bellows. It is a gentle waft you need, not a broadside.

Check for the Queen

If you are not using a queen excluder your queen might be underneath the crown board. If you nonchalantly pull off the crown board and drop it beside the hive, you might lose or kill your queen. So look on the opening sides of everything you lift. She might well be there and she should be coaxed gently into the brood box. This also applies to the lid of the hive and, more usually, the queen excluder.

The Super

I am assuming that you have a super on top of a queen excluder, a super for the colony stores and then the brood box. You might have your queen excluder above the colony stores super if it is full of honey. The queen is not likely to lay in this.

Sometimes the queen is able to get through the excluder and lay in the smaller honey frames. Before removing any top super boxes, have a look at the frames to be sure there are no eggs or grubs in the cells. Should you find either eggs or grubs here then it is possible the queen is also somewhere in this box and you will have to inspect your excluder for breakages. A loose pin at the edge that leaves the grill liable to be pushed up is usually the culprit.

When you remove a super from the hive, lever it out with the hive tool so it becomes unstuck. Do not lift it by the frames but get a firm grasp at the sides of the box and lift with a straight back. Do not lean over and lift as a resulting bad back may prevent you from being able to reassemble the hive.

Queen Excluder

When removing the queen excluder, lever it gently out onto one edge with your hive tool and do not force it with your hands or bang the hive to release the parts from the bee glue.

Inspect the underside of the queen excluder and then lay it aside. If there are a lot of bees on it, shake them off into the hive with a deliberate single sharp movement. Repeat this if they do not come off.

In the Brood Box

First and foremost you are looking for the queen. A gentle waft of smoke will send the bees on the surface of the frames scurrying out of the way. Gently lever the frames and inspect both sides over the brood box so that if the queen falls she will land in the box.

If you can find the queen, so much the better. This is easier if she is marked. Marking has advantages beyond simple recognition. You can colour code the queen to denote her age too.

If you see lots of eggs in cells then you can be sure the queen is there unless there are lots of drone cells, which might mean the queen is running out of sperm. A large number of eggs in the height of the season indicates a healthy colony.

A strong colony has many bees, all of them busy and moving with purpose. A laying queen will be surrounded by workers and you will find each of the frames with a central brood area with capped and uncapped cells. Surrounding this you will find storage cells with capped and uncapped honey. There will also be lots of cells containing pollen that is used for food. These cells are uncapped and usually only one type of pollen is stored in each cell. You will see the orange, yellow and white accumulations, often the work of a single bee.

In new polystyrene beehives the queen will lay right to the edge of the frame because she detects that the hive is warmer and more insulated.

Bee numbers will increase to around 30,000 individuals and, as the queen continues to lay, you will have to make sure there is enough room. Is there enough drawn frame for the queen to continue to lay to maintain the growth of the colony? If not then the queen might leave the hive for a more comfortable position elsewhere. Make sure that there are frames to be made up in the brood box so the colony can expand and that, once the super is full of honey, there is another on the top to be drawn.

Should your brood box be full and you are worried about the amount of space, you can always add a super to the brood box without the queen excluder. This will give the colony extra space. The rate at which the colony increases will depend on the weather and the flow of honey. In a disastrous year the bees will have to be fed, even during the summer!

Rebuilding the Hive

The frame that you laid outside the hive must be returned to its original position so that the box has its full compliment. The hive is rebuilt in the order it was taken down and in such a way as to preserve the bee space. This means that the queen excluder is placed so that the 'gap' or bee space is the right way round. The same goes for the crown board, but you can get boards with a bee space on either side.

When you put anything (super, excluder or another box) onto a box containing bees, first give them a waft of smoke and then gently lay the box at an angle over the frame. Twist it into position with a slow and careful movement. In this way you are much less likely to kill any bees.

Also, before you put a box with bees in it back onto a lower one, check that you do not have a pyramid of bees hanging from the uppermost box ready to be crushed as you lay it down. If so, shake them off and give them a little smoke to drive them away.

Paperwork

A favourite place for keeping notes about the hive is in a plastic wallet attached to the top of the crown board. These notes should include all the various jobs done in the hive and whether or not the queen and eggs and brood have been seen. All the treatments should be noted, as should any dates when new supers etc. were added to the hive.

Harvest Time

This is the time when the honey is taken off and the bees are put to bed ready for the next year. There is a difference between the commercial beekeeper and the amateur. Commercial beekeepers take all the honey from the hive, leaving none for the bees at all. Amateurs normally take all but one super and also leave any honey stores there may be in the brood box. Of course, commercial beekeepers will leave the bees with a large feeder of sugar syrup for the winter.

I personally believe that we should leave a super of honey in the hive. The value of 15kg of honey to the beekeeper in money terms is nothing compared to the value of the that same honey to the welfare of the bees..Honey is vastly better for them than syrup because it has enzymes and health giving ingredients. If sugar syrup was as good as honey, we'd all be eating that instead. So for me I prefer to give the bees a full super of honey and take the rest. In this way the bees get some of the goodness they have worked for. If all they had was sugar I am sure they would know the difference and fly off to get more nectar if it was available.

If you join a beekeeping club you will be able to use their extractor. The comb is decapped and the frame put into a big washing machine like drum which, when full, is spun at great speed thus forcing the honey from the cells. This way you get cleaner honey.

Varroa Regime

You should already be counting for varroa mites and dealing accordingly. Place a piece of paper on your floor and, for a number of days, allow the debris from the hive to collect on it. Then count the number of varroa mites and estimate a daily fall, ie. how many fell each day. If the daily fall is close to 20, then your hive is in trouble and you will need to treat them. If you have between 5 and 10 mites you should still treat the hive anyway to err on the side of caution. Less than five a day should be fine for the winter, but you will need to treat the colony in the spring as the queen starts laying.

How to Treat for Varroa

You really only have two options. In the spring you should put in place an integrated pest management system specifically for varroa. However, if you encounter a high mite fall per day at any time, then you will need to add an approved varroacide such as apistan or bayvarol. The long period of winter when the queen isn't laying is taken advantage of by many to add a chemical to the hive that would otherwise injure any developing bees. This involves applying oxalic acid to the brood combs, though this is not an authorised method of control. Other substances such as thymol are also added.

Other Diseases

If you have been concerned about the numbers of bees in your hive over the summer you might want to treat the bees for Nosema Ceranae, which is strongly implicated in cases of colony collapse syndrome which are so devastating colonies these days. This normally involves adding Fumidil to syrup feed. I suggest using a small feeder directly on the brood, or even a comb feeder. If the bees are ill they tend not to want to climb up the hive to get feed, especially if they have to pass honey to get it.

The overwintering hive is a still affair. You will want to make sure the queen is healthy and there are still enough bees to carry out the reduced daily activities of the hive. Then you will also need to make sure that the structure of the hive is sound for the winter, that it is strapped into position where animals and people cannot push it over and, if you live near woodpeckers, that there is no chance of them tapping through the brood box. I simply reinforce the box with pieces of wood strapped in place. Remember to note down any jobs you complete.

To make sure the hive is safe from rodents, add a mouse guard to the entrance. This is basically a piece of aluminium with bee-sized holes in it. This will keep mice out of the hive. I must confess that the need to do this came as a great surprise to me. Why would a mouse run the gauntlet of angry bees? Perhaps it is further testament to the value of honey.

The first frosts will kill off the drones, if there are any left at the entrance to the hive. Remove any dead bodies; they serve to act as markers to small animals that this is a bee hive. The first frosts should be the time when you forget the hive until spring when the queen starts laying again and you can worry once more about numbers, survival rates and what to do next?

On warmer days you might just see a few bees flying out, but on the whole the bees are doing what they do deep in the brood box in a little ball. Spend the winter inspecting and repairing, where necessary, the integrity of the outside of the hive and making new brood and super combs, flaming and disinfecting boxes and hoping that the new season will be gentle to both bees and beekeeper alike.

Chapter Seven

The Urban Market Garden

Even if you don't want to make your home look like Tom and Barbara's house in the BBC comedy The Good Life there are still some things you can do to your garden to incorporate vegetables and maybe also some poultry and livestock. The garden is the most natural place in the world to make your own food, and it is possible to achieve a high measure of self-sufficiency in even a comparatively small space.

Start Small

Don't despise the day of small things. People with big plans of turning the garden into a food factory overnight often find themselves discouraged by a landscape that resembles the Somme, aching limbs, a sore back and a heart full of disappointment. When you start small you always have the option of going either backwards or forwards with little extra difficulty.

Stealing Space

There are some garden design principles you can use to 'make up' for pinching some land for vegetables. If you are going to grow vegetables you will, however, need to pinch the brightest part of the garden. Make sure there is plenty of sun, without which there will be little point in the exercise.

The soil quality is fairly immaterial because you can always enrich it with good quality compost or well-rotted manure. I have done this myself on sand and a garden mostly composed of peat. You simply add compost year after year and, if it is ideally home grown compost with worms in it, then you will pretty soon have excellent soil.

Disguising Stolen Space

The basic principles of making a garden appear to be something it isn't are simple. If you want to accentuate length, making the garden look longer than it really is, build a path that cuts a sweeping curve from the main viewing point to the opposite corner. The main viewing point is the position from which most people see the garden for the first time, usually either a door, patio or a window. The sweeping curve gives the appearance of length, especially if the path is narrower at the far end. This needn't be a trick. You can easily build a path from the full width of the patio sweeping to just a couple of feet.

If you want to accentuate the width of the garden then opt for zigzag patterns in diagonal straight lines. This way you are breaking the garden into component parts, either by a path, a fence or a small box hedge. Tudor gardeners used this principle to evolve the potager.

A straight path right down the centre of the garden, the original cottage garden design, still has something going for it. Traditionally the cottage garden was designed with vegetables on one side and flowers on the other, but not just any old flowers, and usually consisted of roses, dahlias, bugles, chrysanthemums, delphiniums and big blousy sweet peas.

Very small gardens will benefit from a blind alley – a fence or a hedge that appears to have something behind it. It reduces the claustrophobia of the tiny garden by giving the illusion that it is going somewhere and that there is some more to see just around the corner. This is particularly enhanced if there is a noisy water feature behind the blind. In such a situation you can both see and hear the illusion, although not completely, and you end up with a very tantalising glimpse of something that really isn't there.

Water

Plants need sunlight, air, nutrients and water. You will need water for vegetables all the time. You see, plants are fantastic! They actually use water pressure to stand upright. Not only can they suck a column of water to incredible heights, they also use the hydraulic tension of water to give themselves structure.

When a plant is under water stress, the columns of water in the plant become so stressed that they break. When this happens the plant has to repair itself. Sometimes it cannot repair the broken tissues completely and the plant then becomes prone to infection. If you allow vegetables to dry out too frequently their immune systems become impaired and they fall prey to fungal diseases, often as a result of the accumulated effects of being forced to repair themselves. Also, when the plant repairs the damage of water stress, it does so by setting down woody tissue. In the long run this woody tissue will make your vegetables tough.

Watering Can

Always be ready to use a watering can; they are important! Try to keep a full watering can in the greenhouse or somewhere warm, especially during transplanting time. When you transplant, the plants need to be watered in. If you

Always have plenty of water nearby, preferably rainwater that has run off the roof. But it is no good having to carry water for miles every day. Plan a good water supply into the space you have pinched from the garden, one that you can use easily each day.

use cold water, or worse still, cold water from a hosepipe, you will check their growth so much that it will take 24 hours or longer for them to even think about recovering. Use warm water from a watering can that has a gentle rose attached so that you can soak the ground without actually bashing your newly transplanted plant to death with the force of the flow or freezing them where they stand.

Watering cans are also very important when there is a hosepipe ban in force. While we are on the subject, do make your water available to wildlife too.

I have very few slugs or snails on my vegetables, but I do have a small army of frogs ready to pounce on the little pests if ever they return.

Compost and Garden Fertility

The next important job to do when reclaiming space for vegetables is to make as much of your own compost as possible, so make a space for a compost heap – the bigger the better! You can disguise it by hiding it behind a fence or a hedge or by growing plants in front of it. For any vegetable garden you will need to import large amounts of nutrients into the soil (and thence into your crops).

You will not be able to provide all your nutrients just by rotating your crops and don't expect your soil structure to remain in top condition without compost. The organic rate of addition of compost or rotted manure to fields is 4 tonnes per acre, which equates to a bucketful per square foot! So you should be able to work out just how many buckets you need.

Every organic gardener should know the benefits of compost. Recent research, however, in universities around the world has found it to be even more important than anyone had previously imagined.

Simply pile up all your vegetable matter into a heap and, after a while, it will become hot and within a year you will have a wonderful, dark and sweet smelling, super rich soil. Done properly, compost is the very best recycling you can achieve in the garden. You can use your waste vegetables, peelings, fruit and any refuse from the garden as well as paper, cardboard, teabags; in fact anything that will rot and make life giving compost with the ability to make soil come to life.

Fantastic Filaments

In times past everyone believed that fungi were solely responsible for breaking down plant material and this process was the limit of their usefulness in the garden, but we now know they are more intimately involved with helping plants to grow. Without these fungi some of our crops simply would not grow at all.

The filaments of many fungi grow through the roots of crop plants and into their tissues, helping them to gather water and nutrients from a huge area – a much larger area than its roots would have managed alone. Common vegetables, particularly brassicas, are packed full with fungal filaments that live inside the plant. These are later released into your compost heap, ready to return to the soil.

Using the rotted waste plant material from the garden not only provides nutrients and improves soil structure, it also seeds the soil with important beneficial fungi. Plants grown without fungal filaments do not do as well. If the same growing medium is used year after year without compost, the yields will steadily decrease, even if more than enough chemical fertiliser is used.

For most gardeners there are two types of compost; the kind you buy and the kind you make. The word 'compost' is itself confusing because it is used in so many ways. The material we make in our wormeries and compost heaps is too strong for use directly on seeds and seedlings and should be regarded solely as a soil conditioner. The compost you buy has been specially treated and prepared.

There is a bewildering array of composts for every possible use in the garden. There are different ones for potting, both for trays and modules. Some are peat based and others soil or manure based using a variety of sources such as poultry, horse and cattle. There is compost with vermiculite, with added nutrients, grow bag compost and even a separate one for hanging baskets. The mind boggles!

All this started as a result of the research needs of the John Innes Institute, which regarded compost simply as a medium used for growing plants.

John Innes

From time to time you will hear gardeners say, "Use a John Innes No. 3" for a specific purpose. John Innes was a London merchant who bequeathed his land for a horticultural research centre which opened in 1910. In order that they could accurately compare how plants grow, they standardised the growing media and produced recipes for different composts for use in different experiments. John Innes never sold compost, but many people think it is a brand.

The John Innes Centre produces three compost recipes for sowing the majority of seeds:

John Innes No 1	Sowing large seeds and pricking out the majority of seedlings
John Innes No 2	Potting on young plants into larger pots
John Innes No 3	Final potting of mature plants

Green Manure

Green manures are plants whose main job in the garden is to provide solely for the soil. They fall into several groups: those for composting, those for digging-in and those that fix nitrogen directly from the atmosphere.

They can also be used to suppress weeds when the soil is being left bare for a long period, perhaps over the winter. This also helps to keep the soil nutrients locked in such a way that the rain cannot easily leach them away, as well as suppressing any weeds.

Of course, many green manures also attract pollinating insects to the garden and, just in case you were wondering, you can eat some of them too!

Henry Doubleday started working on comfrey (knitbone) as a crop in the 1800s. It's so rich in nutrients that it can be composted easily to create a nitrate-rich mixture, ideal for tomatoes and most other jobs around the garden.

Comfrey tea is a simple infusion of comfrey leaves, stuffed into an old pillowcase and allowed to soak in water. The rich, horrid-smelling, black ooze that results makes a wonderful organic feed, a perfect boost all over the plot!

Mostly, comfrey comes as plants that should be planted at a distance of around a metre apart. It grows rapidly and can be harvested once the flowers start to appear. Simply cut it with shears to a height of about 20cm above the soil. It'll keep re-growing right through to October/November, when it switches off for the winter. Once comfrey goes dormant for its first winter, cover it with a good mulch of well-rotted manure or compost, and wait for spring.

In its second year it should grow furiously, providing three or four cuts during the season.

Some other useful green manure plants are:

- Brown mustard
- Leaf mustard
- Buckwheat
- Soya bean
- Sunflower (dig in when young)
- Italian ryegrass
- Bird's foot trefoil
- Alfalfa
- Milk thistle

To make your own John Innes composts first of all mix 7 parts of loam (good quality soil), 3 of peat substitute and then 2 of sand.

John Innes No. 1 fertilizer to add per 1 cubic metre of mix.

0.5kg ground limestone,

1kg hoof and horn,

1kg superphosphate,

0.5kg potassium sulphate.

John Innes No. 2 has twice the amount of ingredients except ground limestone, and similarly John Innes No. 3 has three times as much. You will notice these recipes are not organic, but they have worked well for nearly a hundred years.

The Urban Farmer

Autumn Digging

Traditionally we dig over the plot in the autumn and lay manure on the soil, or sometimes dig it in. Green manures can be planted straight after digging so they will germinate before all the warmth has left the soil.

In the spring, a month before planting begins, the crop is simply dug in and allowed to rot, releasing the vital nutrients and improving the sponginess of the soil.

Varieties for autumn sowing include red clover, trifolium pratense. 'Broadcast' or throw the seeds evenly around the soil at a rate of a handful per square metre. They will grow to a height of 40cm and can be mown and put on the compost heap. From late January to mid-February they can be dug-in, at which point they will die and rot quickly.

If your soil is heavy, try tares, which is actually a bean, Vicia Sativa. This plant will grow a little higher than clover, but will also dig-in quite easily. But make sure you dig it in before it flowers to stop the plant producing beans (although these are edible!).

Both of these plants fix nitrogen from the atmosphere.

Spring Planting

Lupin and mustard are both good plants to grow in the spring. They come up quickly and form a ground-covering crop that can be dug-in easily. Bitter Lupin, Lupinus Angustifolius, should be sown like carrots, a couple of centimetres deep and a couple of centimetres apart. Mustard, Sinapis Alba, needs to be broadcast like clover and again, should be dug-in before flowering.

Raised Beds Versus Flat Ground

Only today someone said to me that she was worried about the trend of people growing vegetables in pots. 'Why don't they do proper gardening?' she said. Well, if all you have is a patio you don't have much choice! But wherever you have the opportunity to grow vegetables in proper soil you should take it. Whether you use raised beds or just prepare the earth for planting is up to you – there are both benefits and problems with both methods.

Pros and Cons of the Raised Bed System	
Pros	Cons
Easy to weed	Waste space with lots of paths
Easy to cover or make into cloche	Can hide pests in the walls
Better drainage	Very difficult to change once built
Easy not to walk on the soil	Not so easy to grow certain crops
Easy to plan for crops	Not easy to get tools in the bed
Can have protective walls	
Neat paths	
Can be positioned amongst flowers	

The average raised bed should be no wider than five feet, allowing the user to reach the middle of the bed without walking on the soil. Lots of crops that are also grown on a field scale such as potatoes and cabbages can find it a little cramped in a raised bed. The bed does allow for good drainage, though, and it is easy to enrich surface soil, but it's not so great for deep down enrichment such as double digging.

Of course beds are extravagant with respect to space. For each bed there is an associated series of paths all around, which need to be looked after, kept weed free and, more importantly, pest free. There is nothing more attractive to a snail or a slug than a warm, moist wall covered in soil for part of its length.

The non-raised bed approach is less attractive to the eye, but much more versatile. The only downside as far as I can see is the compunction to walk on the soil – to avoid this I keep a plank handy.

Why Not Walk on the Soil?

Firstly, the boot is the largest spreader of disease around the garden. Clubroot of brassicas is usually caused by a fungal infection that is transmitted by the feet. If you don't walk on your soil there is much less chance of infecting it.

Secondly, we spend a lot of time getting the soil in a fluffy warm crumble called a tilth. If we walk all over it in our size 10s then this lovely textured soil is compacted to a hard pan.

Having a set-aside area for growing that is not delineated by paths and raised beds allows you to plant in all kind of ingenious ways. You can fill the area with one crop or grow in rows and columns. You can grow crops that don't easily fit in raised beds and you can grow in a completely different way next year.

Fingers

One way of turning a flower garden, or even just a grassy splodge, into a productive vegetable garden is to plant in fingers. Simply cut a bed that looks a little like a hand with protruding fingers which move into the more established part of the garden. This gives you an opportunity to grow crops in an interesting way.

In the hand of the bed you can grow potatoes or cabbage, surrounded by broad beans. Then along the fingers you can grow dwarf peas or salad crops such as lettuce or radish. Along the outside of the hand you could grow onions, spring onions and garlic. Of course the rest of the bed can be packed in with marigolds, nasturtiums and small salad leaves.

Imitate Nature

Over time nature crams the greatest variety of plants into the smallest area it can. We tend to do the opposite, with beds and even whole fields filled with just one type of plant. If all there is beneath a flying insect is a plot full of cabbages, it is likely to land on a cabbage! However, if there are all kinds of colours and crops there is a much greater chance that the insect will land on something other than your precious crops and will probably fly a little further on, to where there are easier pickings.

This is the simple premise for having a great diversity of plants and crops in the garden. It also holds true for reducing the impact of slugs and snails. If your lettuces are surrounded by marigolds, and you have some 'sacrificial' hostas at the end of the row, then you are far less likely to have your crops ravaged.

Companion Planting

There are many combinations of plants that are beneficial, but there are a few that are not recommended for various reasons. Garlic, for example, often taints the flavour of peas, beans and some cabbages. There are many interactions between plants in the soil that we do not fully understand. In some cases beneficial fungi are killed off by the fungi of a competing plant and in other cases chemicals from one plant may inhibit the growth of another. In most cases, however, the presence of one plant actually enhances the growth of the other.

Crop	Benefits From	Best to Avoid
Alliums (Garlic, Onions)	Carrots, turnips	Beans
Brassicas (cabbage family)	Marigolds, Rosemary	Onions
Beans	Almost anything	Onions, Garlic
Carrot	Onions, peas	
Lettuce	Carrot, strawberry	
Peas	Almost anything	Onions, garlic
Potatoes	Marigolds, beans	Tomatoes (same family)
Strawberries	Beans, lettuce	All alliums
Tomatoes	Parsley, marigolds	Potatoes
Turnips, swede etc	Alliums, marigolds	

Limitations

The conditions you need to successfully grow one crop are not necessilary the same for another, and this has implications for companion planting. It is not all that practical to grow beans with potatoes, so possibly the best bet is to stick to marigolds and, although you can grow parsley with outdoor tomatoes, you might be hard pushed to keep it under control in a hot summer greenhouse.

The key to companion planting is observation. There is so much we do not know about how plants grow that your observations and experiments are invaluable in teaching you what your vegetables growing in your soil prefer. There is nothing more important than experience, and you have to get on to the plot. You might find that certain combinations are world beating.

If there are plants that you cannot do without, make sure you grow plenty of the following

Marigold

This plant exudes chemicals into the soil which protect precious root crops from nematode attack. Its bright orange flowers attract insects away from crops and then the smell of the leaves drives them away – hopefully onto someone else's plot!

Lavender

Tudor potagers were ringed with lavender. They attract hundreds of insects and provide an antiseptic in the soil. Besides that, they smell heavenly.

Onion

All the alliums go very well with carrots. They mask the carrot scent, so that the carrot root fly can't actually find their target. With a few exceptions, onions go well with almost anything.

Basil

The strong aroma is unpleasant to many pests, from slugs and snails to aphids. Basil grows well with most crops and is an excellent plant to use in the kitchen for so many things.

Radish

This hot root is a magnet for slugs. They are so cheap and fast to grow that it's simple to sow a sacrificial, crowded row between your salad leaves, potatoes and cabbages.

Biological Control

Every garden has its pests and every gardener has his favourite way of dealing with them. A quick survey, conducted inside a couple of garden centres, talking to people who were buying biological control products, revealed that it was generally thought that this was somehow nature's way of dealing with pests, and was therefore kinder than spraying them with chemicals.

The truth of the matter is that some of these products work in very unpleasant ways. Nematode worms invade their hosts and reproduce inside until the animal explodes, or parasitic wasps lay their eggs inside something or other and the grub wiggles about inside for a few days until it has eaten it alive.

The list of biological control products is huge. You can get something that combats almost anything, and there are always extras you can use to make doubly sure. For example, you can buy nematode worms that attack slugs and snails. These can be backed up with other organic methods – beer traps, eggshells, grease bands etc.

One of the clever things about most biological control methods is that they are safe for other prey animals. For example, I have a frog in my polytunnel who has been an old friend for a couple of years. He swallows up a large number of slugs and other pests and is not troubled at all by the dying creatures that have been treated with the application of Nemaslug I make every spring. If I had used slug pellets instead I wonder if he would still be greeting me with a croak each morning.

Perhaps the best, and certainly the cheapest, biological control method is your own finger and thumb. It is by far the most humane way of getting rid of aphids, slugs, snails, vine weevil grubs and the like. There are two problems, however – they need at least eight hours of rest every day and there is usually a long list of other tasks for them to perform. Nevertheless they should not be discounted as a front line method of pest control.

Pest	Product	Information
Slugs	Nemaslug	Nematodes, use from March over 5°C
	Slugsure	As above
Slugs and snails	Organic Bio Stimulant	A garlic based deterrent. It does not kill slugs, just deters them
Vine Weevil	Nemasys	Nematodes, use from March over 5°C
	Grubsure	As above
Aphids	Aphidoletes	Builds a colony of predatory midges
	Aphidius	as above

	Ladybirds and greenfly	Larvae and adults eat aphids
Red spider mite	Phytoseilius	A semi-microscopic mite
	Phytoline	A combination of two mite species
	Control 2000	As above
Scale insects	Scale nematodes	Nematodes need to be kept moist for 24 hrs
	Metaphycus	Parasitic wasp lays eggs into insects
Mealy bug	Cryptolaemus	Australian ladybird that eats the mealy bug
	Hypoaspis	Microscopic mite
	Leptomastix	Egg laying wasp
Sciarid fly	Hypaspis	Microscopic mite

The Big Dig

Modern horticulture started around 12,000 years ago and, in all the years that followed, growing your own food has involved breaking up the soil.

People who dig their plots say that it is because the process aerates, provides drainage, allows weeds to be removed easily and produces a crumbly texture for seeds to grow in. More than this, it is said that digging the soil in late autumn allows the frosts to get in deep to the soil, killing harmful pests and infective agents.

It is an interesting conundrum. All kinds of plants grow in soil that has not been dug for years, but we feel that we cannot grow anything until we have significantly changed the structure of the soil. The answer to this is that nature is wasteful. For every plant you see in the wild more than a thousand seeds never made it to maturity.

In order to increase our chances of success we dig the soil to make the best conditions for seed growth. Even non-dig gardeners break the soil up a little, or grow on compost added to the surface.

Digging Damages

Whenever you plunge the spade or lower the rotating blades of the rotavator into the soil you are damaging it, and this has to be repaired. Worms you chop up, the moisture that evaporates, the structure of the soil, a good deal of its fertility; all these things have to be replaced.

> Conditioning the soil with the application of well-rotted compost is an important part of the whole process.

Disturbing the soil also triggers the growth of seeds that were once dormant, some for many decades. There are hundreds of soil borne seeds ready to explode into life once the soil is disturbed. Hence there is always weeding to do!

Sharp is the Word

One major problem with spades is that people do not sharpen them. It cuts down the effort needed if you sharpen the blade. It is such an obvious thing, keeping it sharp. You need a spade if you are going to 'double dig' the soil. However, you can use a modern rotavator in a stationary position which will dig itself a couple of feet down; all you have to do then is shovel the soil out. This is a good technique if you are going to plant trees.

Another difficulty with a rotavator is that they tend to chop up perennial weed roots, allowing them to grow into yet more weeds. With a spade you can reach down and pull them out while you are digging.

Getting Aerated

Nothing aerates the soil better than a rotavator. You can create the perfect seedbed, a warm looking fine tilth. A tilth is a soil state that is crumbly in texture that does not allow water to puddle and just about holds together when you squeeze it in your hand.

Clearing Grass

An old plot can be comfortably cleared using a rotavator. There are a number of ways of doing it. Cutting through the turf directly and into the soil does give immediate results, but you will need to

The Urban Farmer

pull out the returning grass by hand. You could re-rotavate several times and weed a little each time during a whole season, eventually reducing the grass population. You could simply cover the area with a light proof material once the rotavating is completed and allow the grass to die and compost in-situ. Alternatively, you could use the spade to clear the top layer of turf and compost that and then turn to the rotavator to break up the remaining soil.

Don't underestimate the amount of physical work a rotavator needs. Try to match the machine to the person. I once chased after a lady who was causing havoc on the allotments because her machine was too powerful for her. As her grip tightened on the throttle, the quicker it flew away! But modern day machines are easy to use, light and will fit into the boot of even the smallest car.

The alternative, and one that has been used by generations, is the spade.

All hail the spade	BUT
You can do everything with a spade that you can do with a rotavator	They can be hard work - especially when unsharpened
You can dig and weed at the same time	They are slow and daunting when you have a large area to cover
You have easy access to the whole plot - corners and all!	
You can slice the top from turf and double dig	
They are low tech and work only via muscle power	
It keeps you fit!	
They are low maintenance	

All hail the rotavator	BUT
They are quick, much quicker than manual digging	They can increase perennial weeds
They make the best crumbly soil	They can be cumbersome
They power through soil that might be a little heavy	They need petrol and considerably more maintenance than a spade
Excellent on virgin ground	
Good for incorporating extra fertiliser - such as organic pellets	

Alliums

Everyone can grow onions, or indeed any member of the allium family, of which there is no need to describe the wonderful flavours this largest group of plants in the world brings to our diet. All alliums have one thing in common - they smell. The sulphur laden compounds produce more than just great flavours and aromas, though; they are responsible for health promoting properties.

Know your Onions

Everyone should grow the various different types of alliums; garlic, leeks, shallots and at least two types of onion. Of course we are used to maincrop, spring onions and Japanese onions. These produce a ready supply of onions from late spring to September, and you can probably store them for use in the kitchen all through the year. In bad winters and in the far north this period is reduced and there are frequent gaps in supply.

Onions also come in long day, intermediate day and short day forms. Long day onions will form bulbs when the day is 14 hours long or more. Short day onions will create bulbs when the day is around 11 hours long. By choosing the right type you can get onions to grow earlier in the spring than they would normally have done, and you can create tastier onions too, because they are mature enough to make use of favourable conditions earlier in the year.

You can buy onions already pre-grown. They are the size of a button and you simply push them into the ground in March or April and leave them to grow. I find it best to use a finger to make a little hole first and then force the little bulb into this. Otherwise, when the bulb bursts into life, the roots push the set out of the ground!

Since onions are biennial, living and growing in the first year and flowering and dying in the second, onion sets have already done a year's growth and if you grow them in too warm conditions you are likely to see them bolting. For this reason I tend not to put onion sets in the polytunnel. It is possible to buy specially chilled onion sets that have their flower buds killed inside the plant, and these are bolt-proof.

Prepare the Soil

Although growing onions from seed indoors is a simple process you will at some point need to plant them out and this means having to prepare an outdoor bed. Onions like good soil – well-manured and well-dug, with good drainage and rich in nutrients. Onions aren't very demanding crops in terms of how many nutrients they take from the soil, but they are lazy plants and won't work hard to get at what is there. Onions have traditionally done well in raised beds that have a lot of wood ash dug into them.

Sowing

If you are sowing indoors, keep the temperature at around 20°C and sow the seeds in a moist compost in plastic modules. You can also sow directly into a bed outside in drills 5cm deep. A drill is simply a scrape in the soil.

The traditional time for sowing indoors is Christmas Day, which gives the plants a chance to get established by April so they can be transplanted. But there are other ways. You could start in November and then transplant to a polytunnel in January. The idea is to keep the seedlings warm, well ventilated and transplant them to their growing positions in soil that has had a chance to warm up.

Transplanting

The soil in the bed can be heated by using black plastic for a couple of weeks before you plan to transplant the onions. Simply use a pencil to make a hole and then carefully drop the onion in place, firming with the fingers. Keep the plants at around 10 – 15cm apart in the row and around 20cm between the rows.

Harvest

Onions sown in the spring are ready for pulling in August. Onions that are planted in the autumn will be ready in late spring or early summer. The over-wintered onions will not keep so well as the spring-sown onions. They should be kept dry so that the skins toughen, and then stored. You can store them in dry sacks, nets or tie them to a double string.

The reason for sowing early is that the onion size is directly related to the number of leaves it produces. The more leaves, the larger the onion. Show onions are huge, but have a reputation for having poor flavour. However, choosing the right variety, you can have good-sized onions – not big enough to break any world records – that are great to eat.

Shallots

Shallots are like small onions and are distinguished by their kick! Pickled shallots are the very best pickles you will find and go perfectly with the strongest cheddar cheese and maybe a pint of beer! The bulbs divide at the base and so for each one you plant you get a handful back at the end of the year.

Simply plonk them in the ground like onion sets. Make sure they are firmly bedded in and not pushed up as described earlier. They should be about 15 cm apart and about 25 cm between rows. You can plant them any time between February and April and harvest them from July onwards.

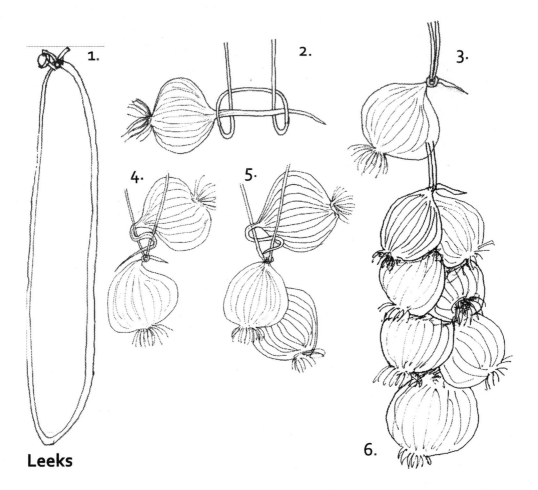

Leeks

Leeks are the most pleasing of plants to grow and in many parts of the North East and Wales they're still grown (in the face of stiff competition) for prize money. All kinds of equipment and 'secret methods' are used to produce the perfect specimens for showing; they are planted in split drainpipes using special compost, drip-fed with nutrient-bearing water and often turned a little each day to keep them growing straight.

'Shirley's Giant Exhibition' will attain a really good girth if you want to use it in a show. It also has generally perfect conformation and the way the leaves splay out from the firm white flesh looks almost like a set of tiles on a Chinese rooftop. But by far and away the best reason for growing leeks is their flavour!

Soil conditions

Leeks are easier to grow than onions because they are tolerant of a wider range of soil conditions. They prefer a rich soil that isn't loose in texture and is reasonably well draining. But you can grow them on clay or sand as well. The only thing that really worries them is water-logging.

Sow the seeds in containers indoors during April or May, or even in a seedbed outside – it really doesn't matter which. By the time midsummer arrives, in late June, they will be as thick as a pencil, and ready for transplanting into their final growing positions. Alternatively, you can buy ready-started plants.

Once transplanted into their final positions, leeks will happily stay in the ground right through the winter, resisting both storms and frost. As long as the soil around them is firm they'll be fine.

and they should be harvested as and when you need them. This can be at any time after they've reached a size where you can't get your thumb and forefinger around them.

Transplanting

People new to growing leeks might worry about this, but it's really easy and the plants respond well to what appears to be harsh treatment!

Flatten the plot (I use a plank that I walk over) and use a dibber – or even a bulb planter – to create holes that are 15cm deep and about 24cm apart. Ideally, the rows should be spaced at 40cm intervals.

Take the young leeks and cut off all but the last 4cm of root and trim the top of the leaves by the same amount. You now have what looks like a bunch of prepared salad onions.

Drop one plant into each hole, then fill the hole with water. It doesn't matter if the water washes a little soil over the roots, all you need to make sure of is that the plants are upright. From this position they will happily grow to maturity.

Blanching

Some people increase the length of the whiteness in the stem by blanching the plants. This cuts out the light to the growing stem and instead of growing green photosynthesising tissue, they remain white. Earthing them up, like potatoes, has always been the traditional method of doing this. Simply use a hoe to draw soil up around the stem. If you don't want the leaves to get dirty then, instead of earthing-up, you can achieve the same effect by fitting collars made from sawn-off drainpipe.

Feeding

These plants do especially well if they are planted in an area where a previous crop has received a heavy load of manure, or following a crop that adds nitrogen to the soil, such as beans. Potash deficiency can lead to increased fungal infection, so a spray with organic fertiliser at the transplanting stage can help. Apart from this, though, leeks require very little care, save the odd watering when the weather is really warm and dry.

Harvest

They should be harvested as and when you need them. This can be at any time after they've reached a size where you can't get your thumb and forefinger around them.

Leeks are always handy for any stews or soups. Simply harvest them as and when you need them, which is usually any time after they've reached a size where you can't get your thumb and forefinger around them. With leeks of this size you will need to loosen the earth around them before you pull them up. But don't deny yourself the pleasure of pencil sized young leeks which are brilliant in a stir-fry, or baby leek mornay is another fantastic way to enjoy the young leeks.

Pests & diseases

Rust: This takes the form of an orange deposit on the leaves and can ruin the plant. It can be treated with an organic copper-based fungicide. Although it's unsightly, it can be eaten or, if you prefer, simply cut away. However, plants that are really badly affected should be burned.

Onion fly and leek moth: In both cases, eggs laid on young leeks hatch to give grubs that tunnel through the plant tissue. Infested plants should be burned.

To counter these two you can cover young plants with fleece until they are well established.

White rot: This is another fungal infection that's promoted by the sort of humid conditions that occur in overcrowded beds. So, to avoid it leave plenty of space in between the plants to ensure that they stay dry. You can recognise this one by the tiny cotton wool-like strands produced. It also leads to rotten bulbs and usually, inedible plants.

Garlic

This is a brilliant plant and one that has served mankind well over the years. For centuries it has been grown all over the world and has been cultivated for its flavour since Neolithic times. It is written about in ancient Indian writings but its use probably predates writing.

By the turn of the millennium garlic was well established in Eastern cooking. Its movement West took many hundreds of years and it only became established in Europe by the late Middle Ages. Its use in Victorian Britain was boosted when some Protestant missionaries from the UK, who didn't eat garlic, succumbed to cholera while their garlic eating Catholic missionaries from France survived the outbreak, although they had drunk the same infected water.

The French have an anecdotal but powerful history of using garlic in a recipe known as Four Thieves Vinegar. In 1721, during the height of the plague, many homes filled with rotting corpses were ransacked by four notorious thieves. They used an infusion of garlic in vinegar and a number of herbs to remain free from infection. One version of the story says that the men were found and executed – so ultimately garlic didn't prove helpful in that particular case.

It did not take long for mankind to realise the health benefits of

The Urban Farmer

garlic, especially its use as a preservative for meats and cheese and that rubbing it on cuts stopped infections. Of course, the medical claims for this vegetable are many indeed and properly conducted 'double blind' medical research has found that many of the health benefits of using garlic are well founded.

Clearly the smell of garlic put people off using it as a food and in India and the Near East the plant was only used as a medicine until around the seventh century. It was believed to inflame passions and consequently all self-respecting people refused to risk eating it.

Garlic likes a good sunny position and grows quickly. Waterlogged soil will check this growth and promote fungal infection. It is important that the soil is well dug before planting and if you can incorporate a spade of sand and well-rotted manure for every couple of feet you will have ideal garlic growing conditions.

Garlic should be planted any time between October and late November and once established it will cope easily with hard frosts. Indeed, the colder the weather, some say, the better the flavour.

Simply break apart the corms from the garlic bulb and plant them upright about 5cm deep in soft soil with the flat end lowest. Cover and gently firm in. This is an important step because, like onions and shallots, the roots will otherwise push them out of the soil.

Space them at 10cm intervals and the rows should be 50cm apart.

Feed them frequently. From April onwards sprinkle well rotted fresh compost, mixed with fertiliser if you like, and carefully hoe it in between the rows. This can be done every two weeks. The plant is full of sulphonamide compounds and, in order to manufacture these, garlic needs a lot of inorganic nutrients. The only other care it needs is to be kept weed free.

It is possible to grow garlic in containers of almost any size. I have grown it in polystyrene drink cups in the past and they worked too, but gave very small corms! They are best in pots of around 18cm filled with compost. Plant them in the same way and water. Keep in a sunny spot but be aware that the compost in a pot gets a lot colder than soil in the ground, so protect them in really bad weather.

Varieties

Cultivated garlic comes in many varieties, each developed with a particular use in mind. In the UK the garlic you buy in the shops, although very cheap, never really does well. This is partly because it is a hot climate variety mostly grown in Spain and Africa. Garlic growers will tell you not to use corms taken from the supermarket – you will always be disappointed. There is a good reason for growing them, however. Because they are cheap I use them to create walls of growing garlic around other crops, particularly carrots. They help to deter pests and then end up in stir-fry dishes – leaves and all! There is little point in trying to store this type of garlic.

Garlic varieties come in two forms. Most of the garlic from the supermarket is softneck, characterised by a lot of corms and papery outer tissue around the neck. Each corm is fuller in flavour than hardneck varieties which are characterised by larger bulbs, a central stalk that is hard and possibly some bulbules at the end of the stalk.

Most of the garlic we grow is the softneck variety, but if you want large corms especially suitable for roasting then a hardneck variety such as rocambole, porcelain or purple stripe are ideal.

There are two main types of softneck garlic - silverskin and artichoke. Silverskin garlic is easier to grow and keeps longer. Artichoke garlic tends to have fewer, larger cloves and a milder flavour.

Elephant garlic is actually not garlic at all. The two major garlics, Allium sativum sativum (softneck) and Allium sativum ophioscorodon (hardneck) are completely different to Allium ampeloprasum which should really be referred to as garlic leek. They make huge bulbs with a garlic flavour.

Ramsons, or Allium ursinum, are the original wild garlic. The whole plant is garlic flavoured and grows in shady, slightly damp conditions. You can smell them from quite a distance when they are in flower and the whole plant is useful in the kitchen.

If you search you will find many hundreds of garlic varieties – here are just a few favourites that grow well in the UK.

Purple Hardneck
Compact tight garlic with a definite purple skin. They are highly flavoured and grow well with few disease problems.

Solent Wight
Good keeping qualities. This will last for a year and still be useable. It has larger corms with a good flavour and can be planted as late as spring.

Chesnok Wight
An ancient hardneck type, probably introduced by herdsmen off the Ukrainian Steppes. It produces attractive rocamboles or floral spikes that should be snapped off and enjoyed either roasted or stir-fried.

Albigensian Wight
A large soft neck white garlic from south west France and grown at the Garlic Farm on the Isle of Wight.

Elephant Garlic
This plant produces a flowering head with cloves often the same size as an entire standard garlic bulb. Each bulb is approximately 5-6 inches across and it can be harvested in July. It is very impressive – even if it isn't a real garlic! It has been described as garlic for people who don't like garlic!

Iberian Wight

A white Hispanic softneck garlic that grows very well in the UK. It produces large corms with a mild flavour.

Harvesting Garlic

When the leaves start to turn yellow in late July and early August it is time to harvest your garlic. Use a trowel to help lift them rather than just pulling on the plant. Get them out of the rain and dry them off in the shed, unless the sun is cracking the flags! If August is wet, get them up and out of the soil quickly or they will start to sprout.

Do not attempt to save any of your garlic for next year's crop. They build up disease and the results from doing this are always disappointing. It is much better to buy new stock each season.

Asparagus

All asparagus varieties, from the aptly named 'Eros' to the royal 'Jersey Knight' have one thing in common. They push shoots up in the spring, some of which we can steal and eat, while the rest grows into a filamentous plant that resembles fennel, in looks if not in taste. It has been grown for over 2,000 years, first by the Greeks and then by the Romans, who valued it both as a food and for its medicinal properties. It's interesting to note that the way we grow asparagus these days was invented by Roman gardeners, and the method hasn't changed in all those years.

Once classed as a member of the lily family, asparagus has the far-reaching and branching root system common to this group but instead of having bulbs, as in the onion, or corms as in garlic, it spreads itself underground by means of rhizomes. A rhizome is an underground stem which grows horizontally, throwing off roots and shoots at various points. Although the whole plant is edible, we only choose to eat the young shoots. Recently, scientists have placed asparagus in a group of its own.

When fully established the modified leaves on this plant make it look like a huge fern and it is very decorative, especially when the rain catches it as tiny beads in the foliage, reflecting shafts of light like little diamonds.

Yielding Results

Asparagus has two sexual forms; the male plant bears pea-sized flowers which are yellow or white and the female has much smaller flowers that are more usually yellow. Some people remove the flowers, giving the reason that they are trying to 'save the energy for the whole plant,' but there's really no need to do this. The main point of interest for us, in the kitchen garden, is that female plants tend to produce larger shoots, or 'spears,' than the male, but male plants produce a greater overall yield.

A bed of asparagus consists of between 10 to 20 plants that, once established, will produce around one kilo of spears per plant each year and this should continue for around 20 years before the plants need to be replaced.

Preparation

When you buy asparagus you will find a tangled mass of roots nestled in compost and attached to a little rhizome that's usually very hard to spot. Jersey Knight can be planted at any time of the year, but it's generally best to plant all varieties in the spring, before the growing season gets underway.

Give the soil a good digging over to improve the drainage and add at least a spadeful of compost for each square metre of soil, mixing well. You can plant the crowns at 20cm intervals with 40cm between each row. There are two common ways of planting the plants, which at this stage are called 'crowns'. You can either dig a 15cm deep trench and lay the crowns at the appropriate intervals, covering them with compost-rich soil, or you can dig 15cm deep holes and plant in these.

Patience

The plant doesn't produce spears that are worth eating for at least a year. It's important that you let the plants grow so that in the second year they can produce stronger spears. They need to be kept well watered throughout the Summer, but make sure that when you prepared the soil you really did ensure good drainage, as standing in water will rot the crowns.

You must also keep the plot well weeded, but this can cause a problem. Indiscriminate use of the hoe might damage the delicate crowns, so weeding by hand and mulching with compost is an important means of control.

In the autumn, from September onwards, the ferns begin to yellow and fall and at this point you can cut them off at the base and put them on your compost heap to tidy your plot. When you have done this, add a good couple of inches of compost to act as a winter mulch. This will keep the weeds down and also add nourishment to the soil.

Harvesting

Most asparagus beds will be ready to harvest sometime in May. It might be a little earlier in the south or well into June in the north.

Never cut all the shoots. With one-year-old plants only pick a third of them and thereafter leave around 15% of the asparagus to nourish the root system for future years' cropping. The time to cut is when the shoots are about 10cm above ground and while the tip is still tightly closed. Harvesting usually continues over about four weeks.

The best way to pick them is with a sharp knife. Hold the spear in one hand and find the base of it just under the soil with the blade of the knife. Cut the spear under the soil, being careful to avoid damaging the crown. It is possible to buy special asparagus knives which have a curved blade, allowing you to pull under the soil to release the spear.

Nothing tastes better than asparagus eaten with butter just hours after it's been picked, so don't wait to use them. The following day will provide a whole fresh crop of spears for you to enjoy, so May-time becomes a serious treat. After harvesting, give the remaining spears an extra feed of organic fertiliser and then make sure they never want for water through the whole summer.

The Urban Farmer

How to Grow a Giant Pumpkin

First of all you need at least two metres around each plant. Dig as much compost and well-rotted manure into the soil as you can; these are hungry plants. Sow 'Giant' seeds in May in pots and keep them warm and moist. Use a propagator and keep them at 25°C.

In June you can plant the seedlings into their growing bed. Place a plastic lemonade bottle over them to keep them warm. You can remove this after a week or so. Water at least once a week, with soluble fertiliser. As they grow, draw soil around the plant to encourage more roots to grow. In July it will flower and produce fruit.

If the stems get tangled or tight, cut some out. Keep on watering and feeding, otherwise the fruit will crack.

Pests

Varieties produced since the Second World War have built-in resistance to asparagus rust. This is a fungal infection that looks like brown spots or smudges on the growing stems. You rarely get this problem these days, but a spray with Bordeaux Mixture or another organic copper-based fungicide protects against most fungal infections.

If the shoots turn yellow early and the outside of the stem is nibbled all the way round, you've had a visit from the asparagus beetle. This is a rare event, but the beetle and its grubs eat the stems and the leaves. If this happens, do not compost the dying leaves. Burn them. Similarly, burn the surviving leaves at the end of the year. Hand-pick the beetles off the crop as they appear in spring, which should keep them at bay, but you could spray with an organic insecticide to be on the safe side.

Artichokes

Artichokes of all kinds are worth growing just because they look good, never mind the health benefits that can be derived from eating them, including blood pressure benefits and the reduction of cholesterol. They are basically big thistles and we eat the bracts on the fruit. They are perennial and prefer a well drained sunny spot. There is a lot of debate about the best time to eat them, but just before they open is best. They are easy to grow from seed, but take up tp 5 years, so most people buy them as ready to grow plants. 'Green Globe' is the favourite.

These are big and dramatic plants and will grow 1.5 m high and at least as wide and they live for over 10 years, so the site you allocate them is important. Each year give them a good deep mulch of well rotted compost and in the summer a sprinkle of good quality organic fertiliser.

In the first year remove all the chokes (young flowers) and let the plant build up its strength. In the second year only allow a few to develop. You cut them off with a little stem, or pull them away with a snap just as the bracts begin to open, but don't leave it too late.

Aubergines

It is important to grow these indoors unless you are able to guarantee a sheltered spot that has a constant temperature of 20°C for their easy growth and good fruiting. They are members of the potato/tomato family and require similar conditions.

Varieties

Old favourite varieties such as 'Black Beauty' and 'Moneymaker' are the traditional appearance and are probably the most popular. There are a number of other shapes and sizes making this a fun crop in the greenhouse or polytunnel.

Cultivation

It takes almost all summer to grow an aubergine, so get them off to a good start in the early spring. Sow them in trays at 20°C, not too wet but humid. If you can guarantee draught free conditions and a constant temperature then leave the lid off the propagator. When the second leaves appear, transplant them into pots of compost.

They grow slowly and will take 10 weeks to reach the size where you can transplant them to rich, fertile soil that is well drained. They should be 45cm apart.

Like Tomato

Well, in a way! When the plants are 15cm tall, snip out the growing point to encourage the side shoots, of which you need 4 or so. Feed them like tomatoes with tomato fertiliser at least once a week and don't let them get too dry at this stage. From late August onwards the fruit will be ready for picking. .

Keep the humidity high and make sure you have an effective means of controlling the aphids and red spider mite, which seem to be their major pests.

Beets

Beetroot contains betaine, a relaxant, and is used to treat depression. It also contains trytophan, which is found in chocolate and contributes to a sense of well-being.

This is such a wide ranging plant that it almost defies description. Most people think of beetroot when confronted with beet – but the sea beet was cultivated first by the Greeks, then taken over by the Romans who made it into many other varieties.

Beets are easy to grow plants and can be grown in most soils and beetroot in particular provides a great root with leaves you can eat. The soil can be fairly sparse in nutrients. You can even grow beets in a bed recently used for a previous crop without adding any extra manure or compost.

Some people say the seeds of beetroot should be soaked in water first, but if you are sowing in May this should not be necessary, especially if the soil is moist. Water the drills both before and after sowing.

The seeds are actually a number of seeds stuck together and these will produce a number of seedlings. The secret is to sow them thinly into drills about 5cm deep.

As soon as the seeds are growing you can thin them to allow the plants to grow freely, firstly to 5cm between plants and then a hands width. You can cook the thinnings or use them in salads.

Beetroot will ball up if there is plenty of room between plants, but if you leave them alone they will simply increase only as far out as their immediate neighbour. I haven't tested this theory, but if you don't bother to thin the plants I wouldn't be surprised if you got the same yield, but they may well be fairly useless, ball-less plants. These will be quite good for feeding to hens and pigs.

Leaf Beet

You get some wonderfully coloured green and red plants from beets that grow either in pots or beds. You grow it in much the same way as you do beetroot and the plants grow large bright leaves. You can boil them or eat them raw and they are great fun to grow.

They prefer a richer soil than beetroot and homemade compost is beyond doubt the best ingredient. The chard can be sown at 5cm intervals with 45cm between rows and left so that the leaves grow large together – at least a hand's-width. The first thinnings are a bit like a crop in themselves. You can harvest these plants more or less any time you are hungry and if you successively sow new rows every two weeks you should have them in the soil until October at least.

Broccoli

These are fairly easy to grow. They can be sown in modules – I use little drinks cups with holes in the bottom for drainage.

One tip my pal Phil McCann gave me was to sprinkle rock salt around the plants, avoiding the leaves, in the middle of summer. This mimics the seaside aspect of their ancestors and does help produce cracking plants.

You can sow indoors in April, but some varieties need to be sown earlier and others later, so it is important to make sure you read the instructions on the packet for your particular variety.

Be careful when you transplant them. The calabrese types do not transplant well, and this is the reason for growing them singly in cups, because you can get them in the soil with little trouble or damage to tender roots.

To avoid clubroot, see the cabbage section. But don't grow broccoli where you had cabbages last year.

Plant them about 60cm apart and firm them in well. They don't mind any soil really, but perhaps prefer it slightly on the wet or heavy side. Choose a spot that will not be waterlogged in the winter.

They do not like being dry, so make sure they are watered well in times of drought. As they grow to about 30cm give them a good mulch of rich compost and a feed of organic fertiliser.

You can harvest the plants when the flower heads are ready – not beginning to open, but good and tight. Taking the flowers will mean that the plant will produce more – this is the archetypal cut and come again plant.

Broad Beans

Beans have been grown in the Old World for thousands of years and remain one of the staples of mankind. Mentioned in the Bible as being used to feed the escaping King David and his army, beans had already been grown for 7,000 years in the area, particularly in Egypt and Syria. From here they spread into central Africa, Spain, Italy and southern France. It took 8,000 years for the broad bean to actually make it to Britain because our climate meant that growing it needed some lateral thinking, but the Romans managed to work it out.

In Egypt the bean is sown in December, flowers in February and is harvested in June, but in Britain harsh winters and millions of hungry molluscs meant the crops frequently failed. The Roman answer was to plant the beans in the spring. Roman horticulture was heavily dependent on the gods and the phases of the moon and stars and this 'discovery' represented a departure from so-called superstitious growing and was a direct result of scientific observation. Later, the Saxons discovered that if you started beans before the winter you could coax them through the worst of the weather and get an earlier crop.

Broad beans are also called Fava beans (Vicia faba – nice with a drop of chianti!); and belong to a different genus from other garden beans (Phaseolus), and can be used in several different ways in the kitchen. The most common way we eat them here is as fresh beans taken from the pod, but you can also eat the pods whole when young, and the tips of the new shoots too. Alternatively, if you wait until the pod turns black they can be harvested and used as dried beans and store well.

Habit

Broad beans come in two types – Longpods and Windsors. The Longpods are said to be hardier, give higher yields and crop earlier, whereas the Windsors supposedly taste better but have a lower yield. I suggest sowing both types; Longpod in Autumn for early cropping and a Windsor-type in the early spring. Then you can make your own mind up about which you prefer!

Broad beans vary in height, from the large 1.5m (5ft) varieties such as 'Imperial Green Longpod,' down to the dwarf 30cm (12in) types such as 'The Sutton.' There's a difference in how long these plants take to germinate and then to fruit. Germination can be a little haphazard, especially if the seeds are kept too warm. The general rule is around 16-weeks from germination to fruit, but the autumn-sown varieties take longer, although they do tend to crop more heavily.

Care

Broad beans are usually easy to grow, whether you do it the Roman or the Saxon way. They don't need a lot of feeding and will happily give a good crop in soil that's been previously manured for an earlier crop, say potatoes.

They do however need a free-draining soil, especially the autumn-growing varieties. They do fine on medium loam, but if it's heavy, full of clay or too wet they tend to rot. On lighter soils you might need to stake the plants.

Legumes and Nitrogen

Broad beans are members of the 'legume' family, which uses soil-borne bacteria to convert gaseous nitrogen in the atmosphere into ammonia.

The process is called 'nitrogen fixation' and is part of a cycle that sees nitrogen being taken from the air by bacteria and undergoing changes, allowing the plant to utilise it during growth. When the plant dies and is composted, the fixed nitrogen is returned to the soil, thus enriching it.

This cycle only works efficiently if the right bacteria are present in the soil. These 'fixing bacteria' invade the plant and its response is to make nodules – usually on the roots, in the case of legumes – where the process takes place. Generally these bacteria are plentiful, but if you sterilise your soil you'll kill them and nitrogen fixation can't occur.

The 'returning' of nitrogen to the soil only works if the plant is allowed to rot down, either in a compost heap or directly where it grew. Alternatively, you can cut the plants off at ground level and leave the roots behind; these will quickly rot and enrich the soil. This is especially effective if you can rotavate the land to break the roots into small pieces. If you pull legumes out of the ground after cropping you will leave behind a more deprived soil because the plant is taking with it the naturally-occurring nitrogen in the soil that it utilised while growing.

Autumn Sowing

You need a well-drained soil that will retain a little water, but not too much. Cold water chills the seedlings, so they grow very slowly. Having said that, bean seeds of all types prefer cool conditions for germination.

The soil needs little preparation and you can grow them where a previous crop has been cleared – ideally potatoes. Some people add a little fertiliser to the soil, but I tend to wait until spring because I don't want to encourage too much shoot growth at this time. Simply give the soil a dig over and mark out your double rows.

Broad beans are grown in double rows. That is, each row is made up of two lines of seeds, planted 15cm apart. The next double row comes 75cm away from the first.

Make a small hole with a dibber and push a seed into each at a depth of 5cm and cover it, firming the soil down. Germination, which might take three weeks, will follow with growth to about 10cm. At this stage they will appear to stop growing. They haven't actually stopped growing though and are actually sending out a complex mass of roots and this is what promotes heavy crops later.

You can protect them from the worst of the weather by covering them with some fleece and be on your guard against slugs and snails. You won't need to water them, but some people earth them up a little with a small draw hoe, carefully avoiding covering the leaves. This encourages surface rooting and helps conserve moisture.

In the spring, hoe down the centre of the double row and at the same time add a little organic fertiliser. As the temperature warms the shoots will grow rapidly and the tenderest parts might just be susceptible to black fly. However the plants will be too well-established to be bothered too much.

These can be harvested by May, the earlier the better because as the beans dry they become tough, so pick them as soon as the pods fill.

Spring Sowing

The Roman method can be more fraught. Many people start them off in February in the greenhouse and find they don't germinate too well. This is because they're too warm. Having said that, if you sow them directly into the soil the combination of pigeons and mice – both of them ravenously hungry at this time of year – will make short work of your young seedlings.

The Urban Farmer

I prefer to sow into plastic drink cups and keep them on the floor near the door of an unheated greenhouse where they remain cool but protected. Once the plants are large enough (10cm) they are planted into double rows as for the previous method.

The bed should have been previously well dug and a little organic fertiliser mixed in to give them a good start. I usually use a handful of organic fertiliser to a metre length of double row.

Before you finally plant your young beans out, leave them out of the greenhouse during the day and take them inside again at night for a couple of weeks – except in driving rain or hard frosts – to acclimatize them to the outdoors.

Dig a hole with a trowel that will accommodate the root ball and firm in well. A small amount of rainwater will set them off, but don't over soak them.

Pests

We have already mentioned pigeons and mice, but beans can also be attacked in December by slugs on their final drag around the garden. However, the main problem for broad beans is blackfly, which is an aphid. The bean becomes tough from the bottom up and the aphid can't penetrate the outer skin except for at the tender top. Most gardeners pinch out the top 15cm of the plant once it's set fruit, leaving only the tough plant behind. This does deal with most of the blackflies. They also congregate on the tubules of the seed casing, leaving poor seeds inside. A jet of water removes most of them, or use an organic insecticide or a soft soap solution.

Broad beans are susceptible to a fungal infection that leaves dark patches on both leaves and fruit, but the seeds are seldom touched so you can eat them anyway – but don't save them for re-sowing.

Brussels Sprouts

As members of the cabbage (brassica) family, sowing and planting Brussels sprouts is done in the same way and so, to avoid pages of repetitious material, please refer to the cabbage section because they have the same basic needs. However, they do not completely follow suit. If they are not firmly planted they will produce loose sprouts that are hardly worth the name. So from time to time it is a good idea to put your boot on the soil around the growing plant to make sure it is firm.

Firming the soil prior to the onset of winter is most important. If the plants are very tall, you might want to give them additional support by using stakes.

Cabbage

The wild cabbage, sometimes known as the sea cabbage, has an interesting distribution around the UK. It is frequently found on the south coast, and within a few miles of a Roman fort or town. Indeed, this so called wild plant was introduced by the Romans and is just another garden escapee, but one of great antiquity. Now anyone who tries to tell you that cabbages are a difficult crop are rebuffed by the wild cabbage – if it has lasted for sixteen hundred years around the country after the Romans have left, then it must be really easy to grow. It is easy to worry about cabbage because of this, but there is no need.

Constant Cropping

You can sow and harvest cabbage at any time of the year. It takes between 20 and 32 weeks after sowing, depending on the variety you use, to produce a good cabbage, but you don't really need a good cabbage for a meal. You can grow cabbages in pots and they will grow like a Roman candle, but you can pick off the leaves and boil them up just like any other, or put them raw in a salad.

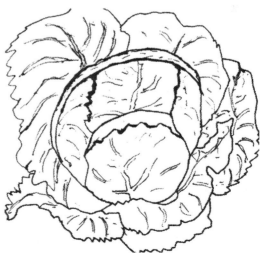

The Urban Farmer

How to Grow Cabbages

There are basically two ways of sowing cabbage; direct or transplanting.

You can sow cabbages directly into the soil in which they are going to grow. Sow thinly in drills that are 5cm deep and 60cm apart. Cover and firm in. This way you get a lot of seedlings and these need to be thinned out so that you get healthy plants around 45cm by 60cm from each other.

This method uses a lot of seed, so the idea of growing in a seed-bed and transplanting the young plants to their final growing positions caught on. A seed bed is a finely prepared bed where the seeds are sown. Once the plants have four good leaves and look sturdy, they are carefully pulled up and transplanted to their final growing positions. The seedbed can be a bed in the garden somewhere, or more usually these days, a tray of individual cells, called modules.

A Cure for Clubroot

Cabbages suffer from a fungal infection that distorts the roots and stunts the growth of the plant. Clubroot, Plasmodiophora brassicae, works mostly on young cabbages and is slowed almost to a standstill in lime. So you can grow cabbages in 8cm pots and then dig holes in the soil to receive the plants once they have grown up somewhat. Each hole can be given a good handful (wear gloves) of lime. You will not get rid of clubroot, but this will help an awful lot.

Soil

Cabbages need good, rich soil that has been well dug into a fine tilth. It needs to be easy draining, but must hold some water. The way to prepare this is to dig in a lot of well-rotted manure. A dressing of organic fertiliser will give the young seedlings a further boost.

Hearty

If you grow cabbages in cramped conditions they grow like spears, consequently cabbages in pots grow straight into the sky. You can still use the leaves, as we have already said. Give them room and the leaves will form a ball, or head. The minimum space to create heads is around 45cm.

Care

As the cabbage grows, some of the leaves die off. These should be removed because they can promote infection. Keep them weeded with the hoe, but once the leaves begin to touch there is no need to continue this. They will benefit from a dressing of fertiliser about two months into growing. A good mulch of well rotted compost is ideal.

Try not to let the plants dry out and once they are established they will only need watering in times of drought. Split cabbages are caused by a lot of watering after a prolonged dry period, so keep the water evenly available. You can cloche cabbages grown through the winter, especially if it is very wet. Some people earth up their cabbages like potatoes, but this is something I have never tried. It is supposed to help with frost protection.

Pests

Birds, caterpillars and cabbage root fly can be avoided by using a fine mesh. Some people use discs of carpet or any barrier available and lay it around the plant so that the fly cannot lay its eggs at the root. Whitefly and mealy aphid are also a problem but can be dealt with by using an organic insecticide or a jet wash of something like simple soap to keep them under control.

If you have any problem with your cabbages and you have to pull them up, do not compost any infected material and when you move around the garden, keep your boots off the soil, taking care to only walk on the paths.

Cabbages are troubled by caterpillars. I have found the best way to keep this under control is to cover the growing plants with fine mesh. But, and it's a big but, I always grow one or two that are open to the skies because butterflies need food too!

The very best way of growing good cabbages is to keep the nutrient content of the soil high. Plants have their own immune systems and if they are given a rich soil they will grow to be very healthy.

Harvesting

Cabbages can be pulled at any time. You can eat all of it, even the roots, but they will be a bit tough. If you grow cabbages in different seasons you should have them available every week of the year.

Cabbages All Year Round		
Autumn Queen	Sow in June	Harvest late autumn/winter
January King	Sow in spring, early under plastic	Harvest from December onwards - also works for November sowings
Minicole	Sow from April to July	Harvest from October onwards
Caramba	Sow from February indoors to June	Harvest from June to November
Pixie	Sow from summer through to autumn	
Rodeo	Red cabbage - sow in spring	Harvest in late summer. Needs to be pickled for storage

Cauliflower

Traditionally these are viewed as difficult plants to grow in that people tend to find them a little disappointing, but they needn't be so daunting really. There are two types, summer and winter, and you can have crops all year round if you like.

In a way the difficulty comes from their soil requirements. You have to plan ahead. In the winter decide where you are going to grow them. You will need a rotation for them and add well rotted manure and a decent amount of lime. Leave this to settle before mixing it in with the soil to make the bed. You need a fine tilth which is ever so slightly alkaline.

You can sow indoors in a propagator in modules ready for transplanting. Sow under a moderate heat – no warmer than 15°C. You can also sow outdoors in April using a cloche to protect the plants. Outdoors sow at a depth of 3cm and the rows should be about 30cm apart.

Summer caulis grow quickly and they need never dry out. They also like a lot of nutrients, so once a month give them a sprinkling of organic fertiliser – I have even watered them with tomato feed before today.

When the heads are forming you can fold over the leaves to protect them. I do like to take them early, but continuing feeding will produce a very much larger head.

The problem is that they tend to come all at once You can do a little successional sowing, but not very much. They do, however, freeze well, so make sure you have a deep freeze. Alternatively, you can make piccalilli with them too.

Carrots

Carrots go back to prehistory and are found on pyramid wall paintings. They were brought to the UK by the Romans, though there is some evidence that they were already here. At the time, some 2,500 years ago, carrots were yellow or white, but not orange. By the Middle Ages the carrot was all kinds of colours; black, red, green and purple. Then, in the 16th Century, Dutch growers found a yellow variant and created the orange carrot as a patriotic novelty by a series of interbreeding experiments.

As the British Royal family became linked with the Dutch at the time, orange carrots became popular here too and consequently everyone thinks that carrots are orange! Black, white and purple carrots are now making a comeback onto British seed lists.

Carrots are members of the Umbelliferae family, also known as Apiaceae or bee flowers, of which nearly all species are useful to mankind. They are biennial, growing and storing food in the first year and producing seeds in the second. If you leave your carrots in the ground over winter they will flower in the spring and produce seeds that may be viable for certain varieties.

These colourful roots are packed with health promoting chemicals such as alpha carotene in orange carrots and beta carotene in purple carrots. All colours of carrots come with an impressive range of health benefits which do vary slightly according to colour, but vitamin A is present in good quantities in all varieties. They are also packed with almost every other vitamin we need. Carrot juice is an excellent way of taking these nutrients, but don't drink more than a glassful a day because your liver will not be able to cope and you might just start turning orange.

Carrot types

There are three basic types of carrot: Danvers, Imperator and Nantes. There is also a cross type called Imperator-Nantes. Danvers carrots are the standard summer Chantenay carrot. Summer carrots are frequently prefixed as 'Chantenay' and, although it's confusing, these are all Danvers carrots.

Nantes carrots were developed late in Victorian times in France to create a smaller carrot for canning. They are often sown in early spring. 'Early Nantes' is a typical and very common example.

Imperator type carrots are more modern and very high yielding. This makes them the most popular type of carrot for growing.

Growing carrots

They prefer a light, sandy soil, enriched with well-rotted compost or leaf mould. They don't need much in the way of compost and land manured for a previous crop is ideal. For this reason they are frequently grown after potatoes. Sowing something like 'Autumn King' directly after the potato harvest will give a crop anywhere between Christmas and February.

If your soil is heavy then you might consider growing the ball-type such as 'Early French,' 'Rondo' or you can dig a trench and fill it with sand/leaf mould (or compost) mix, or choose to grow carrots in containers that are about a foot deep. Some of the best carrots are grown in this way, and you can sow in October if you like, indoors in a good container, knowing you will get a crop in February to March.

You can have carrots all year round if you sow them in succession at different times of the year. You can start in late January and continue through to August and you should have carrots more or less ready for eating in every month of the year.

How to sow

The key for growing carrots is in the preparation. They have a very sensitive growing point and if this comes against a stone it will divide into two tap roots. Consequently, you will get all sorts of oddly shaped roots in unprepared soil. The most important preparation is done with the hoe. You simply cannot hoe the soil enough. Remove any small stones and make the soil as light and fluffy as possible, to a depth of at least 30cm.

Make a drill about 10cm deep and as long as you like and sow the seed thinly. One seed every 4cm in spring and one every 10cm in autumn/winter. This extra space allows carrots grown in cooler days a chance to grow to a decent size more quickly. If you are sowing in autumn, lay some plastic on the ground to allow the soil temperature to rise, and cover with a cloche. Temperature is critical for speedy germination, which should be complete in around 12 days.

Cover the seeds loosely, tapping down only enough to stop the soil from blowing away. Water them as the soil dries, but don't drown them. Carrots lose their colour and rot in wet soil.

As they grow you will need to thin them to around 8cm apart – although autumn sown carrots will need no thinning. Please don't throw the thinnings away – cook them in a stir-fry or use them in salads!

Weed by hand if possible. Carrots don't do well when they have to compete with weeds. They become thin and don't lay down starch in the roots. The major problem is carrot fly, which appears from late spring to early summer. They can smell carrots for miles around and simply fly 'upstream' of the concentration gradient of carrot aroma. They lay their eggs at the base of the carrot and the maggots then eat out the carrot. They only fly at a height of around 50cm, so if you build a barrier taller than this they will never actually get to your plants. A simple 'wall' of horticultural fleece will provide a good enough barrier against these pests.

A year-round supply

Jan – February

Sow 'Early Nantes' or 'Thumbelina' seeds under cloches. These will grow to become your first crop around May.

March – April

Sow 'Baby Bell,' 'Early Nantes' or 'Amstardam Forcing' which will crop in July. Also sow any of the 'Chantenay' types that will mature in August.

April – May

Sow your main crop carrots; 'Mango,' 'Manchester Table,' 'Jumbo' and 'Resistafly' (which implies this has some carrot fly resistance).

August – September

Repeat sowings of 'Amsterdam Forcing,' 'Early Nantes,' 'Thumbelina' or 'Autumn King.' The August-sown plants should be covered with straw in the cold weather and the later ones treated to a cloche. These should provide carrots from Christmas onwards.

Companion planting

Carrots do well with garlic and onions, especially if you want to mask the aroma of carrot from the dreaded carrot fly. They don't do well with other root vegetables such as parsnip and turnip close by. A Victorian method of sowing carrots is to put them into bunches around the garden, instead of rows. A bunch of five or six carrots, evenly spaced, will grow happily inside wigwams, amongst lettuces, celery and potatoes – almost anywhere. You can work out how many meals of carrots you need and plant up the appropriate number of bunches.

Growing show carrots

We don't normally get involved in showing, but this novel method of growing can provide some whoppers. It isn't usually the thickness that counts but the length; a single, long tapering root that hasn't snapped off or split. The world record is something like five metres. You too can get close to this if you wish by using a drainpipe, sawn in half lengthways and taped together. Fill it with a sieved mixture of sand and a little compost. Sow the seed in one end and feed them with general liquid fertilisers. Every other day turn the drainpipe so that the carrot grows straight down. (You may have to site the pipes on a slant, depending on their length).

When it's time to harvest, simply break open the drainpipe and wash the sand away – you will have an unbroken carrot inside.

Harvesting

You can leave carrots in the ground. You have to beware of slugs in the winter, but I simply cut away the bits of damaged carrot and eat the rest. Wash them in cold water and dry them with paper towels. You can store them in boxes of sand where they will keep for ages, or you can put them in airtight bags and freeze them or pop them in the fridge – where they will remain moist.

Celeriac and Celery

You more or less grow these two plants in the same way. They both need the same very rich soil and they are both started off in mild heat in late winter. Celery needs to be sown in March and you can sow celeriac seed from mid-February to mid-April, both at about 15°C. You need to transplant them into small 7.5cm pots of multipurpose compost.

When all possibility of frost has disappeared, plant the seedlings out 30cm apart with 40cm between rows. The soil should be rich, with a lot of well rotted manure and compost incorporated, a little like potatoes.

Never let your plants dry out and, from time to time, give them a general purpose liquid feed. They will be ready for harvesting from early autumn to late spring. Celery sticks are sometimes earthed up to keep them clear and white.

The Urban Farmer

Chillies, Peppers and Capsicums

Chillies and capsicums are becoming more popular these days and are often grown alongside tomatoes in the greenhouse or polytunnel.

The heat of a pepper is measured on the Scoville scale. It is a huge, numbered scale that isn't always that helpful, but a mild chilli would be around 100 – 500 and the very hottest would be the Naga Jalokia at about 855,000!

Sowing the Seeds

Sow in February in the greenhouse in trays of compost. Carefully pat the compost down until firm and wet the surface with a spray. Sprinkle the seeds on this, cover them with a little more compost, pat them down again and spray on a little more water. The temperature should generally be over 21°C. At the two leaf stage you can pot them on in stages, first an 8cm pot, then a 15cm pot and finally a 25cm pot.

From now on you are more or less treating them like tomatoes, feeding them a couple of times a week. There are not that many problems with diseases but they should be kept free of aphids, white fly and red spider mite.

The fruits are ready when you either see a colour change in them, from green to red or, in the case of capsicums, when you view them as big enough to use.

Courgettes and Marrows

These are sort of interchangeable, but courgettes are now bred to be at their best when 10cm long. They are sown outside in mid-May to be sure of no more frosts. If this is not possible use a cloche. Dig a hole about a spade deep and as far around and fill it with good quality compost. With the soil you dug out, mix in an equal amount of compost. Make a mound on top of the compost and plant 2 seeds in this. These should be watered in. There should be at least a metre between plants.

Pick out the worst growing plant and allow the best one to grow on. Water if the weather is dry and feed once a month with a liquid feed (I use tomato feed). During the summer the plant will grow strongly and produce male and female flowers. You can tell female flowers by the fact of the ovary behind the yellow petals. You can pull off the male flowers and pollinate the female ones. From now on the courgettes will develop.

Water slightly away from the centre of the plant and do not let the leaves get too wet because they are prone to fungal infection. The more frequently you take the fruits, at around 10 cm, the more flowers will appear.

Outdoor Cucumbers

For ease of growing and reliability, outdoor varieties can't be beaten. They can cope with low temperatures and do not need any support, but the fruits are more likely to be straighter if the plants are supported.

Sowing

Sow in individual pots, 2-3 seeds per pot and about 2cm deep. Sow in late spring to avoid the risk of late frosts. Do not over water the seedlings, but pinch out all but the best growing plants. Once the plants have at least two 'true' leaves, they can be planted into their growing positions.

Add plenty of compost to the soil and make a little hill into which you transplant your cucumber. They like high heat and humidity and some people mulch them with straw. They are ideal plants to grow not far away from a pond. Keep them well watered and feed them with tomato feed at least once a week.

Once the fruits are produced, pick them as soon as they are useable. If you let a cucumber mature, the plant will stop production.

Kale

Kale is another brassica, is very hardy and very easy to grow. They have few pests and birds seem to steer clear of them. You can pick and come again and this crop will last a long time in the ground.

They are grown just like cabbages, so refer to that section. There are several varieties and all hold well right through the winter. The flavour is just like all the other greens, but perhaps a little stronger.

Lettuce

You can eat lettuces every day of the year if you like. The year probably starts in December in the greenhouse, when you can sow them indoors. They need a minimum of 10°C to germinate and grow and require plenty of moisture. That said, they grow very well in the winter in the greenhouse and a sowing on Christmas Day can be eaten in March, although they will grow more slowly! You need to sow lettuces indoors right until May and then sow them outdoors.

Transplanting lettuces

This can be really hard! The problem is that their leaves tend to grow big but their roots are under developed and this makes them difficult plants to transplant. The roots can be damaged in the process and they wilt off. For this reason they are better grown wherever you start them off.

Sowing

Simply mark a groove in the soil or compost about 2cm deep and lightly sprinkle the seeds in place with the finger and thumb. Cover and water the young seedlings and protect them from slugs. As the seedlings grow, thin them out by pulling alternate ones. Don't waste the thinnings; use them in a salad!

Make sure they do not dry out, but try to water only the soil, not the leaves, and watch out for greenfly. I usually kill them with my thumb.

If you start sowing in June, repeat the sowing every two weeks until the end of August. The seed packets say stop in July, but it doesn't cost a lot to get an extra month in and, in the middle of September, cover them with a cloche. (I use upturned and cut off lemonade bottles.)

Parsnips

Parsnips are fantastic plants to grow. Related to carrots, they were the Elizabethan standard vegetable, eaten more or less exclusively by the poor. It is an easy plant to grow, except that it takes all but a year to mature. They are very hardy and are actually better flavoured if the frost gets to the roots.

They prefer a neutral to alkaline soil and one that isn't overly rich in nutrients. Well, actually they love rich soils; it makes them grow like mad, but the roots are usually all divided and useless for the table. Unfortunately, they are a little like carrots in that stones and excess nitrates make the taproots divide up or grow into strange and impossible shapes. You can sow them any time the earth isn't freezing.

I think you'll agree that the seeds are actually little aliens in space ships. Well, that's how they look to me, and I could be right! Before you sow, prepare the soil. In early March dig the soil and remove any stones. Give a good dressing of lime and hoe it in. You are looking to create a fine tilth. Make a 2cm drill and sow the seeds 5cm apart. Cover and leave them to germinate, which can take as long as three weeks. Rows of parsnips should be 50cm apart.

As they grow, thin them to 20cm and cover with a barrier as for carrots, because carrot flies like parsnips too, though parsnips are less prone and a little early for this particular pest.

Try to keep them weed free and do not damage the plants. Any wound can be a source of infection. They are prone to parsnip canker when they go all brown and rusty looking.

They are also troubled by a number of pests, notably wireworm which causes them to go mushy. Generally speaking, though, they have few problems, save the need for water in their early stages and during any dry periods.

You can leave this crop in the ground as long as you like. Once December arrives look out for frosty nights, which will be improving the flavour of your parsnips. These plants are biennials so, if you leave them for the second season, they will flower and seed. It is worth keeping one or two if you can for the seed, and also for its splendid appearance.

Peas

You can grow peas in so many ways; in containers, drainpipes or virtually anywhere.

Many people don't know that the humble pea comes in two basic forms – a bushy, low-growing type and a climbing vine. In recent decades, peas varieties have been selected to become progressively smaller and closer to the ground, which is useful for harvesting, especially if you want to grow them in a huge field and collect them with a combine harvester. We tend to forget that peas were originally climbing plants and it was this type that took Europe by storm over two hundred and fifty years ago.

Preparation

Prepare the soil by digging a trench 30 x 30cm and fill it two-thirds full with compost, old newspapers and vegetative kitchen waste and then backfill with soil. As this waste matter rots, it will produce heat and the fibrous material will store water. By doing this you'll be able to mature your peas in the heat of the summer without having to worry too much about drought. Climbing peas will need a support, possibly a trellis or net, so site them where this will be possible.

Sowing

Peas can be sown into their growing positions in December-January and over-wintered under cloches to give them a head start. This will give a first crop in early May and, if you make weekly sowings, it's possible to have a continuous crop all through the summer and right into late autumn.

Sow in lots of three, with 25cm between sowings, in rows at least 50cm apart – although some people prefer to keep them 1m apart. Alternatively, they make ideal wig-wam crops, planted against canes.

Once sprouted, select the strongest shoot to grow on, removing the two weaker plants. Seeds sown in March will be ready in May/June, while those sown in August will be ready in late September. Once they have reached 20cm/8in they can be under-sown with lettuce and marigolds to fill the soil where the three will happily coexist.

General maintenance

Keep the plants well watered, but make sure they aren't left standing in any excess. Once they start flowering, don't disturb the soil at all as even a small amount of hoeing will cause the petals and any forming fruit to fall off. Check regularly to make sure the plants have enough support. Remember that this climbing variety will grow fast!

Harvest

Pick when the pods are full and plump and the peas are tender. Hold the vine in one hand and pull the ripe pod up and off with the other. This variety takes 75 days from sowing to cropping. The pods are edible but not that nice, but the wrinkled peas are the sweetest you'll ever find. In the unlikely event that you don't eat them all immediately, they can be frozen or dried to give a supply during the winter.

Problems

All peas are susceptible to 'damping off' and fusarium wilt which are both fungal infections. These can best be avoided by making sure the plants aren't under stress and have enough water, but at the same time, not too much. A well-drained soil is best.

Powdery mildew can also pose a risk, but this can be treated organically by spraying with Bordeaux mixture, available from all garden centres.

Aphids might be a problem, but there are a number of organic remedies available, ranging from the 'finger and thumb' method (see page 112) to spraying with a soft soap solution.

Potato

The potato, brought back from the South Americas in Elizabethan times, has been worth much more to this country than the many tons of gold that came over in the same ships. The original tubers bear little relation to the ones we grow these days, but the plants have been grown in much the same way for 300 years.

Two Types of Spud

There are basically two types of potato, waxy and floury. Floury potatoes are used for mashing and frying or roasting. Waxy potatoes are used wherever the texture of the flesh needs to remain intact; mainly for salad potatoes and boiling.

A Bit of Science

A waxy potato has very strong cell walls made of cellulose that tend to stay intact during cooking. A floury potato has weaker cell walls that burst open easily. Once the cell walls break, the escaping steam within the cell causes an explosion of starch. When fried this fluffy starch becomes crispy.

The time needed for the plant to produce a reasonable crop is important. 'First Earlies' need around 12 to 15 weeks, depending on where you are in the country. 'Second Earlies' need 17 to 20 weeks and 'maincrop' need 20 to 25 weeks.

Skin quality is also an important factor in the distinction between maincrop and earlies. You could dig up a maincrop potato in July and get a crop of small potatoes that would have a decent(ish) flavour but with a chewy skin. Alternatively, you could leave a 'First Early' in the ground to get bigger tubers, but they would fall apart much more easily in the pan.

You don't want a baking potato the size of a conker, and it clearly takes longer to make a big potato than a small one. The golden rule is to stick to what it says on the packet and that way you will not be disappointed

First Early Varieties
Maris Peer, Home Guard, Arran Pilot, Pentland Javelin, Rocket, Pink Fir Apple

Second Early Varieties
Kestrel, Wilja, Estima, Osprey, Nadine

Maincrop Varieties
Admiral, Cara, Eden, Maris Piper, King Edward

Preparing the soil

Preparation of the soil is important. It must be like a sponge and full of well-rotted organic matter. Potatoes need a lot of water, but apart from in emergencies this water must come from the soil itself. Incorporate as much organic matter as you can some weeks before planting – even during the previous winter.

The Potatoes

Do not save potatoes from last year. They very quickly gather viral problems. Similarly, you should not plant potatoes bought from the supermarket. You can get new 'seed' potatoes for around 20 – 50 pence each and they will guarantee the very best results. From each potato you will get around £2 - £3 of potatoes, probably even more.

The main UK potato varieties can be graded according to their waxiness

1 Waxiest
Nadine, Pink Fir Apple

2
Cara, Marfona,

Home Guard,

Sharp's Express

3
Estima, Wilja, Saxon,

Nicola, Charlotte,

Kestrel

4
Maris Peer, Maris Piper,

Romano, Desire

5
King Edward, Sante

6 Flouriest
Golden Wonder

Chitting

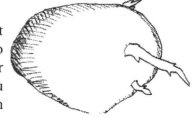

This is what the potato does for itself. If you leave them in a light, airy space, enzymes will start to convert the starch to sugar. As soon as this life giving substance hits the dormant buds (known as eyes) they will burst into life. Victorians used to think that the shoots produced from chitting gave the plants a head start. This is not always so. Recent research has shown that chitted maincrop varieties might have storage problems later. The truth is that un-chitted potatoes will go through the same process under the ground anyway.

Planting Method 1 - the trench

Dig a trench a spade's depth by around 10m long. Simply lay your potatoes, eyes uppermost, in the trench and cover. Earlies should be spaced 45cm (18 in) apart and maincrop 75cm (2ft 6in) apart. Maincrop rows should be 75cm (2ft 6 in) apart and Earlies rows should be slightly narrower.

As the plants grow they will soon appear out of the soil and, at the roots, tubers will form. These tubers frequently appear at the surface. Use a draw hoe to pull earth up around the stems so that the tubers remain snug under the surface. Potatoes exposed to light become green and consequently contain a high level of alkenes, which will at best give you a tummy upset and at worst make you quite ill.

Planting Method 2 - straw

Non-dig gardeners can grow potatoes on the surface. Make a ring of straw and place a seed tuber in the centre. Cover it with straw and douse with water. As the potato grows, cover it with straw and a layer of compost. Continue to add straw and compost until the potato is well established at around two feet high.

Continue to add compost around the outside of the plant until it becomes impractical because of the foliage. This system will need careful watering.

Planting Method 3 – a plastic bag

This works best with Earlies.

You can grow potatoes in bags of compost. Put a black lining inside a plastic shopping bag so that no light can penetrate it. Loosely fill it with compost and puncture the bag for drainage. Insert the tuber into the bag and wait for growth. When the vine appears out of the bag, tie the neck to keep out the light. This will need watering weekly.

Planting Method 4 – a pile of tyres

Start with two tyres and fill a liner with compost. Water weekly, but in high summer you might need to water every other day. As the plant grows, add more compost and, when needed, another tyre up to a maximum of four.

Potato care

Potatoes grown in soil should not need watering unless there is a real drought. In the summer they will set flowers and eventually fruit. These should be removed if at all possible. Since the soil will have been well fed before planting, no extra feeding should be needed.

Harvesting

Remove the vine of only one plant and use a fork, digging away from the vine, and lift the tubers out of the ground. When you have the majority of them, dig deeper to remove all the tubers, no matter how small. They must not be allowed to grow next year; otherwise disease will build up in the soil.

Potatoes can be left in the ground – there should be no need to lift them all unless you need the soil. They can be stored in airy, dark conditions. You can clamp them by digging a hole and lining it with straw, piling your potatoes inside, covering with more straw and then soil to seal.

The Potato Clamp

A few feet underground the temperature is fairly constant and burying root vegetables in a clamp is a good way of storing them - as long as you mark where the clamp is, that is! Dig a hole as deep as you can manage . A depth of 75cm should be your minimum aim and at this depth you will avoid an unwelcome influx of water. Line it with a good amount of hay and pile your dry, cleaned root crops on top of this. Cover them with at least 30cm more of hay before piling the soil back. The temperature in the clamp will never freeze or become too hot, so you can leave them there until you need them. It is also very rare for any animals to get to them either.

Diseases

Potatoes get more diseases than almost anything else in the garden.

Blight
Potato Blight is caused by a fungus and appears on warm days following rain. When you see black splodges on the leaves, dig them up and spray the remainder with organic copper based fungicide. It is best avoided by giving the plants plenty of aeration by not having rows of plants too close together.

Scab
This looks like little brown scabs on the tuber. It has no real effect on the crop and is simply peeled away.

Eelworms

These are microscopic worms that turn your crop into a nasty soup. They reduce yield and can really only be tackled organically by good rotation.

Wireworm

Wireworm is the lavae of the click beetle that lives on grass. Your crops are only really at risk if they are grown on new plots that were once grass – so don't bother for at least a year following clearing.

Crop rotation

It is best if you do not grow potatoes on the same piece of land for four years. This gives nature a chance to remove any diseases. The well manured land is ideal for growing many other crops.

Radish

Originating in the Far East, radish have travelled the world and become popular because they are easy to grow, tasty and versatile. They are, in fact, so easy to grow that many children cut their teeth on growing radishes of all sizes. They only take around 50 days to produce edible roots and can be planted at almost any time of the year.

At one time a radish was a little red ball vegetable that was hot when you bit into it. But now they come in all shapes and sizes and are huge fun to grow. There are many varieties of radish, but the following are representative of them all.

Winter Types		Summer Types	
Mino Early	Long, cylindrical shape, white body and easy to grow	Saxa	One of the earliest radishes that has perfectly round roots with deep red skins and crisp white flesh. Stays fresh for a long time after harvesting
French Breakfast 3	Crimson body tipped with white. Crisp, mild and flavoursome	Sparkler 3	A round radish with a very red skin and a large white tip. Great in salads, being crisp and peppery.
Black Spanish	An excellent cold weather variety which will hold its growth over the coldest days to produce a good spring root		

Radish will germinate in almost any soil and grow well in almost any temperature. You can sow them in November if you protect them with a cloche, or you can grow them in the polytunnel.

Plants grow to around 30cm in height with large, sometimes warty leaves that are lime green in colour. The leaves are completely useless for eating – not that they are poisonous, they just taste bad and are rather tough! However, the young leaves are fantastic and can be picked for salads or used in stir fries.

The root swells quickly into its final shape, some long and cylindrical, others the traditional round ball. The ball types are referred to as summer radish while the cylindrical ones are winter. This is a little misleading because you can grow either type at different times of the year.

The name radish comes from the Anglo-Saxon for red, which is fairly obvious since most of them are red. But you do get green ones and others that are all white.

How to sow

Radishes like full sun but do best in cool conditions. This paradox is typical of the brassica family of which radish is a member. You have to remember they grow very quickly and, if you go on holiday, or are not able to eat the whole of your crop, being fibrous they quickly become too mature to eat. Ideally in the summer you need to sow every two weeks.

Sowing in winter

Sow a variety like 'Black Spanish' into modules in December and keep them in a cool greenhouse. In March, plant them out and then follow on with a sowing directly into the soil a couple of weeks later.

You can also plant directly into the soil in November and cover them with a cloche to heat the soil with whatever warmth the day brings. You have to be careful of bolting if you plant them too early. This can be avoided by keeping them frost free and using bolt-resistant varieties. You might have a crop for December in a warm year, but the leaves will be edible while they are young. Of course you can plant them in a polytunnel at almost any time.

Sowing every couple of weeks in late spring and summer will keep you in radishes until late autumn.

As with carrots, make sure your soil is well fed and finely worked. They prefer a well dug, water retaining soil which has plenty of nutrients. Make a drill and sow the seeds at a rate of around one per centimetre. Cover them and water. If you are growing more than a row at a time they should be about 30cm apart.

As the seeds germinate – and you should expect near 100% success – the leaves will peep out of the soil and you can take every other plant in the row to ensure a decent sized crop. Those you have taken to make room for the others can be used in salads and stir-fries; they are certainly much too good to waste!

You can sow radish anywhere, alongside other plants, with beans and parsnips being favourite combinations.

Care

Radish are truly plant and forget plants. They really only need to be watered and more or less frost-free. Because they are so quick growing they present a novel answer to pest control. Since there are always a few more on their way, so long as you grow them around the plot, if something goes wrong, what does it matter? Just pull them up and wait for the next lot!

Perhaps that isn't a really good answer to the problem of radish pests! They do suffer from most of the problems encountered by other brassicas. Flea beetle, cabbage root fly and slugs and snails are the worst culprits, and probably slugs and snails are the biggest problems. They do get clubroot, but respond well to a well-limed soil.

Rhubarb

It was impressed upon me that rhubarb leaves are poisonous when a kindly but misguided neighbour threw all his off-cut leaves into my chicken pen. What a mess! What those leaves did to my birds' insides doesn't bear thinking about and it took weeks to get them right again.

The concentration of oxalic acid in rhubarb increases as the summer continues and by the height, sometime in August, you should leave well alone. Never take the leaves. You will end up with the quickest 'runs' imaginable and have stomach cramps worse than being kicked by a horse. To top it all, your liver will have had the equivalent of a few dozen pints of beer.

Having said that, rhubarb is fantastic. It is easy to grow and one of the few 'sweet vegetables' in the kitchen.

Soil

Rhubarb will grow more or less anywhere as long as the soil is free-draining. If the soil becomes waterlogged you are likely to lose the crown to fungal infection. Try to place it where there will be no shade. Rhubarb is a hungry plant, so dig in plenty of well-rotted manure and compost.

Make sure the spot is free-draining by adding plenty of grit and stones to the bottom of a hole at least 60cm deep, which is then filled with a soil/compost/manure mix. Each spring enrich the soil with a good few spades of well-rotted manure.

Planting - from seed

Sow in pots of compost in late winter in a warm greenhouse. I let the seedling grow until it's looking like a well-established plant – which could be May – and then transplant it to the final growing position. Protect it from slugs.

Planting - with crowns

The most common way of obtaining rhubarb – unless you have a good mate nearby who is willing to give you a crown in the winter – is to buy crowns. These look a little like a big red bud on some dead looking roots. Simply bury the whole thing in the soil with the roots down, and cover it so that the bud of the crown is a couple of inches below the soil level. Give it a good drink of water and leave it. This can be done in winter if you like – the plant at this stage is already quite hardy.

Care

The plant looks after itself, more or less. All you have to add is plenty of water through the summer. Remember, any crop that has large leaves has an equally large capacity for water even though it doesn't like to be waterlogged. Cut or pull off the stems as they come to a decent size any time from early April. By June the plant is at the height of its production and, before the end of the month, stop cutting. It's important not to take all of the stems. The crown (the central growing point of the plant) needs plenty of nutrition, so leave five or more leaves on throughout the summer months. In August give it another mulch with compost. Weeding has to be done on all fours with a trowel. Rhubarb doesn't tolerate soil disturbance, so get in close. Do be careful as a misused hoe can cause cuts in the plant that may lead to fungal infections.

Forcing

You can do this in a number of ways – particularly cleanly by putting a pot over the growing plant. You will get thin, long, sweet stems. I must confess to not really liking to do this for the following reason. The exaggerated growth of the plant comes at the expense of food from within the plant's reserves and not from sunlight. To my mind this puts the plant under stress – something I try to avoid so that the plant is healthy enough to avoid disease.

Ready for harvest

It takes a good season's growth before the plant is ready for harvesting. Start the plants off in the spring and then start to harvest in the early summer of the following year. Your plant will be productive for around a decade if you continue to feed and keep it weed-free.

Dividing

After around five years of production the plant can be divided, usually into two or three parts. In the winter, when the leaves have dried back, dig the plant up and, with a spade, cut between the many crowns to create equal sized portions. These can be put back into the soil or kept dormant in a terracotta pot of compost over the winter and then planted into a prepared spot in the early spring.

Completely bury the crowns, roots downward, so that the top of the plant is around 5cm under the soil. Mark this place until, in the late spring, the new plant bursts forth.

Diseases

Rhubarb suffers from few problems except rot. Bruise the skin when the soil is wet and you'll be in for problems. Crown rot is a fungal infection that will kill the whole plant. With rhubarb the important part is the crown (growing in the middle of the leaves). Damage this and you've lost your plant. There's no effective answer to crown rot except to dig the plant up and burn it.

This problem is best avoided by having the soil as free-draining as possible and leaving the plants alone – the fewer bruises they get, the better.

Spinach

As long as you keep this warm it will germinate and produce a decent crop. Sow in a long line on the outside edge of the polytunnel in October/November and you'll get a crop of baby leaves. They might grow to a larger size or they might not, but you will have enough for salads all the winter through.

Apart from that you can sow spinach like cabbage, outside in the late spring and then every couple of weeks until the end of summer and have greens all the time. They are not too particular as to the soil, but will accumulate nitrates even to a dangerous level, so do not over feed it.

It requires little care. Simply sow it in rows that are 45cm apart and as the seedlings grow, thin them to 25cm between plants – maybe a little more. Don't forget to eat the thinnings.

Swedes

Swedes are odd creatures – they are basically cabbages with funny roots. In fact, if you chop up a cabbage root, cook and eat it, you will see the resemblance. As a brassica it has the same problems as the rest of the family, notably clubroot. Imagine a swede with clubroot! They prefer ordinary soil but are not that fussy at all. They will grow better from seed if you add some organic fertiliser to the soil a couple of weeks before you sow them. The major problem is that they do not like their roots being damaged and so dislike being transplanted.

The swede is longer in the ground than a turnip and has a greater flavour (well I think so). But turnips grow quicker and are available earlier. So from Easter onwards, put turnips in the ground for successive crops and have swedes growing for a late autumn and winter crop.

Prepare for sowing much the same as for parsnips and sow the seed in late April to early May. The seeds are sown at the same rate and rows should be 60cm (24in) apart. You can grow them in plugs indoors in late March and then plant the whole plug without disturbing the roots – in this way the plants get a good start. Do not try to transplant them, it never works! Thin the plants progressively to about 60cm (2ft) and use the thinnings in cooking.

Apart from greenfly and cabbage root fly they do not really have any problems. They can get mildew if too wet and there is, of course, clubroot to consider.

Swedes, also known as Swedish turnips, take about 20 weeks to grow. If you sow in May you should start to have a crop in November. You can leave them in the soil as long as you need, and the frost doesn't really cause them any problems. Twenty plants should last at least until late March or April. Simply lift the plants as and when you want them.

The Urban Farmer

Sweetcorn

As soon as it's picked, sweetcorn starts to convert the sugars it contains into starch, so the only way to get the very best is to grow it, pick it, run up the garden and cook it! A few decades has seen corn on the cob move from something eaten only by Americans or cattle to one of our favourite summer crops.

Zea mays, or maize, is believed to be South American in origin, although some think it may have its roots in the Orient. It's been spread around the world by mankind and has been cultivated for at least a thousand years. It's actually a gigantic grass and reinforces the fact that the greater bulk of human food is provided by this family of plants.

There are three keys to growing sweetcorn: it hates any form of cold, it doesn't like root disturbance and it is pollinated by wind like all the grasses. Corn should be an important smallholder's crop – especially in towns and cities. Cobbett argued in his Cottage Economy that everyone should grow it, and if it was possible to grow this crop two hundred years ago, it should be possible in the UK today because it is slightly warmer now than then. You can feed pigs, goats, hens and people with corn, so you should plan to grow a lot.

Soil

Sweetcorn hates clay. Normally, a well-worked clay soil is good for growing because you can always guarantee a water supply, but since sweetcorn likes it hot, it hardly ever germinates in a clay soil where the temperature seldom rises above a few degrees. So, a well-dug soil with plenty of nitrogenous organic matter will produce the best plants.

Start early, digging the soil in January or February and incorporate plenty of well-rotted compost. Cover it with black plastic to inhibit weeds and allow the soil to heat up. Worms and micro-organisms will 'settle' the compost/soil mixture and by the time you set your plants or seeds it'll be in perfect shape.

Season

In the UK the temperature rarely rises high enough for corn to grow as well as it should and consequently it needs a long season to fulfil its potential. For optimum fruiting you need to get started as soon as possible to give the plants plenty of chance to flower.

You can start them off in a greenhouse and transplant the. The seeds can be sown when there's no chance of frost. You can either hope for the best or you can eliminate the risk by growing them in a polytunnel – especially in the north.

Starting off

Usually, sweetcorn is started in a heated greenhouse in March or April. Use peat pots with good quality compost. Sow two seeds into each pot, avoiding the temptation to soak the seeds. They will germinate in a week or so if the temperature is kept above 12°C and the compost is moist. Once growing, pinch out the weaker of the two plants.

When May arrives, gradually harden the plants off and, after a week, they can be planted out into the prepared soil. Plant the whole pot (break up the bottom of the pot a little if you can) and firm it in carefully with your boot. As the plants grow they may need support. You can stake them if you like, or as an alternative, draw up soil around the growing stem. This is a worthwile precaution against the wind as they can't bear root damage and excessive rocking can damage them.

They will do better if they are covered but if you can get a cloche over the young plants all well and good. Transplanting will cause a check to growth and the plants will need to be cosseted.

The further south you live, the better chance you have of simply planting the seeds in their final growing positions. You will need to prepare the soil as above and in late April or early May (you will know yourself the possibility of frosts in your area) sow the seed and cover with a cloche.

The Urban Farmer

Grid

Since sweetcorn is wind pollinated you need to maximise the chances of full heads by making sure the breeze carries pollen to all your other young cobs. To help this, corn is grown 60cm apart in a grid rather than in rows. Consequently you need to grow more than a few plants; otherwise the wind might just blow the pollen away without doing its job. A good number of plants are 20-25 in a block a couple of metres square.

Growing

An early feed of nitrogen-rich compost gives the plant a good start for vegetative growth, but flowering and seed production require potash, so a feed of tomato fertiliser every couple of weeks will be beneficial. Avoid the temptation to put a barrier around the plants to 'keep the pollen in.' Pollination needs a breeze, without which you will have a poor crop.

If you're growing corn in a polytunnel, use the grid method as above and open the doors to get a breeze going on hot days once the filamentous flowers appear. It's best if you can open both ends of your greenhouse. If not, try to grow nearer the entrance.

The developing head is protected by thick leaves which are enough to keep most pests away. Sweetcorn is remarkably free from disease. You might just get a rust on the leaves caused by puccinia, a fungus, but there's no cure and it doesn't usually upset the plant.

Harvesting

Sweetcorn needs sun and heat for a long time. From mid to late August you can test the fruit. The further north you are the longer you will need to wait. Pull away the protective leaves and thrust your nail into one of the seeds. If it oozes a creamy white liquid like milk, the head is ready for picking. A watery ooze means the cob needs more sunshine.

You should pick and cook it straight away. Cobs will keep, but the longer they're kept, the worse they taste.

Varieties

New varieties of sweetcorn appear as F1 hybrids, which produce excellent results, but don't try to save the seed because they won't come true and some might not even germinate at all. The further north you are the shorter your season, so try early varieties.

Ambrosia F1	Highly attractive and early to mature, making this an ideal UK variety.
Indian Summer F1	The first sweetcorn to produce multi-coloured kernels with a top quality flavour
Tuxedo F1	Sugary and grows up to 2m
Golden Bantam	This is the archetypal corn on the cob corn
Strawberry Popcorn	A tiny variety producing a large number of little heads - ideal for making popcorn

Sunflowers

The reason for growing this plant should be apparent. You can make great bread, extract oil, feed hens and livestock and they look good. It is a member of the Jerusalem artichoke family and is really easy to grow. Start them in modules in spring and put them in a rich soil that is not too dry and in a sunny spot. I like to line the garden all round with them. For every plant you grow you will get 500 seeds – 2 handfuls, and a chicken will eat a handful a day. So you could grow a couple of hundred of them all over the place – on spare lanes, around allotments – in fact anywhere.

Once planted they only need supports and a little tomato feed during the summer. Their main stems make brilliant compost; all in all a really worthwhile plant to grow.

Tomatoes

For a main sowing in mid-March, use small module trays of either moist seed or multi-purpose compost. When sowing several varieties of tomatoes, then 9cm pots each with 3-4 seeds is a better option. The seeds are sown evenly then lightly covered with either a fine layer of compost or fine grade vermiculite. Vermiculite can help prevent 'damping off,' a fungal disease affecting young seedlings.

Place the trays or pots in a heated propagator (20°C) and germination should take between 5-14 days. Once the young plants have reached about 10cm in height, they can be moved to an open propagator or a sunny spot for a week or so to acclimatise them to their final environment.

Cover them up with fleece overnight, particularly if frost is forecast. Then they can be potted up into 13cm pots and placed on a bench, ensuring they receive enough light so they do not have to stretch. Planting your tomatoes directly into the polytunnel soil can be carried out from early April onwards. Continue to monitor the risk of frost, covering the young plants overnight with insulating material such as fleece or bubble-wrap.

Water the plants in well initially, then let them dry out slightly to encourage root growth. Water them lightly until the first truss appears, then water them more heavily and start feeding using a liquid manure, seaweed or comfrey liquid at weekly intervals.

Top tips for success

- Try planting French marigolds 'tagetes' next to your tomatoes to deter whitefly.

- Remove side shoots regularly on cordon types.

- Keep the doors closed at night to preserve heat.

Varieties

There are so many varieties available and why not ring the changes by growing a couple of 'heirloom' varieties too? The range of colours, shapes and sizes will certainly add interest to your summer salads!

Golden Sunrise (indeterminate)	An old variety, introduced in 1896. Golden yellow fruits of medium size, excellent flavour with a thin skin
Tigerella (indeterminate)	Very early cropping. Full of flavour and very attractive red fruits striped with gold. Can be grown in the polytunnel or in a warm spot outside

Harbinger (indeterminate)	Another older variety dating back to 1910. Described as 'one of the best flavoured tomatoes, with a smooth, thin red skin. A classic flavour lost in many modern types
Roncardo F1 Hybrid (indeterminate)	Early beefsteak. High sugar content resulting in better flavour than other beefsteaks
Tornado F1 (determinate)	Produces a heavy yield of red, cherry sized fruits with excellent taste and texture

Training

Tomatoes are grown indoors as cordons. Outside they are generally grown as bushes. I wonder why we call the way we grow tomatoes cordons because this term refers to the way we grow vines along wires in rows, with the branches splayed out and supported on wires. What we tend to do with tomatoes is quite the opposite, taking out all the side shoots that appear between the leaves and the main stem.

The old fashioned way of growing tomatoes in the glasshouse was to let everything grow, side shoots and all and tying the branches to wires like a proper cordon. This tended to give more plant per square foot of soil, but proportionally not that much more fruit. Also the size of the fruits were smaller until around 1830 when market gardeners began to build large glasshouses to feed the growing towns, and consequently started to demand more economical use of their expensive buildings.

Two ways of growing tomatoes were developed from this, which we took around the world. In the UK we now remove the side shoots until we have five or six flowering trusses. Then we remove the growing point (the very top of the plant) to stop the production of any new flower trusses. This ensures that the fruits have the chance of growing as big as they can without having to struggle for nutrients with too many competing trusses.

Growing Side Shoots

A lot of research has been done to see if it is possible to grow new

The Urban Farmer

The ideal way to grow tomatoes in a tunnel is to plant directly into the soil. Prepare the planting site by digging in plenty of well-rotted manure or compost. Space out the plants at least 25cm apart and decide how you will be supporting them as they grow. Traditionally, bamboo canes or similar upright supports are used, but strategic positioning of the plants under the polytunnel hoops means they can be supported by string attached to the frame itself.

tomato plants from side shoots. It has been found that a mixture of 50% sand, 30% perlite and 20% compost (or peat substitute) is the ideal growing medium. Reduce the leaf area of the side shoot with scissors; place the shoot in the mixture in a 15cm (6in) pot and water well. Within a couple of weeks you will have another plant.

Alternative Training

The other way we used to train tomatoes still takes place in the Far East. This is to take out the growing point of the plant as soon as a side shoot appears. Tie this to a stake and allow it to grow until a truss appears and another side shoot grows. Take out this growing point and allow it to grow, stopping and training until the plant reaches six or eight trusses. If you are feeding with a rich fertiliser, plants grown in this way can be grown very large indeed with some commercial varieties reaching well over a dozen trusses.

Watering and Feeding

Drip feeding tomatoes with water that has a measured amount of nitrates in it is done commercially to provide maximum fruit growth without building up the nitrates in the soil. However, in a domestic system this is not all that easy. You could buy liquid feed but you will need to know exactly how much feed is added to the system. In this way commercial growers get nearly 100 tonnes per acre of tomatoes.

You can use a watering system to drip

four times per week from a reservoir system that has home made fertiliser made from comfrey or manure. Once the tomatoes have finished you can mop up the residual nitrate from the soil by growing potatoes or spinach.

Diseases

Leaf curl is often a function of the feeding regime or climate. In some cases it can be due to a virus. Usually the crop is not affected, but the application of a good all round fertiliser on top of any other system you have can abate this.

Aphids are another problem for which you will have a favourite cure including the fingers, soft soap sprays and any number of organic insecticides. It is important to remove these because they can encourage other diseases including viral infection.

You can usually tell viral problems because the plant reacts in unusual ways. Yellow patterns to the leaves, misshapen leaves and fruit are all typical. Destroy these plants by burning them.

Blight is mentioned elsewhere in this issue. It is important to remember that tomatoes are the same family as potatoes, and do suffer from this problem.

Finally, the main problem people get is blossom end rot. This is why the tomato is called the 'cow of the greenhouse,' not because it is a difficult plant but because it must be tended regularly. Blossom end rot comes at the back of the flower, and consequently the fruit, when watering is only done on an irregular basis. You will not get it if you water copiously and regularly.

Emmer

English

Bread Wheat

Durum

Chapter Eight

Urban Wheat

In The Sunday Times on 24th February, 2008, Johnathan Leake announced that the world was ten weeks away from running out of wheat, the lowest supply for 50 years. And there is still time for wheat to become even more expensive before the first harvests around the world increase supplies. If bad weather ruins yet more harvests there will be real problems next year. The supply of wheat is suddenly becoming a political as well as a nutritional hot potato. China and India are buying more wheat than ever before and now have the financial muscle to outbid us in the global markets. Growing wheat now doesn't seem such a daft proposition.

In Victorian rural England, wherever a farm worker had an allotment it was invariably used for growing wheat – vegetables were grown in the back garden.

Actual yields of wheat vary around the world according to the ambient temperature, the local weather, disease and fertility. On average you get between 1.5 and 4 tonnes per acre. A convoluted set of simple mathematics on the back of a beer mat show that this kind of yield translates to a day's bread being obtained from about a square metre to two of garden. So, if you can dedicate the land of an average sized allotment to growing wheat, you will have, more or less, a year's supply of flour.

Now, who can say they have made their own bread from their own wheat? And you get a lot more than wheat! You get straw too! But you don't get this without some hard work.

The study of the development of wheat from its origins in crops like emmer and einkorn that were grown as early as 8000BC (and are still grown today) to modern short stalk wheat, is fascinating. Its impact on human development is also amazing, allowing a huge increase in numbers, effectively facilitating language, trade and prolonging our ancestors' lifespan.

Getting Wheat Seeds

Wheat is not the kind of seed you find on the front of a gardening magazine. Indeed, you can only buy it from certain agricultural suppliers. The smallest bag of wheat you can get is 25kg and this is more than enough for an allotment. All wheat comes with a DEFRA number on the packet which allows the final product to be traced. It is a way of controlling certain diseases. Some wheat is coated with anti-fungal agents and these are dyed red so the seeds are not easily put into the human food chain themselves.

Non-Bread Wheat

There are many types of wheat strains developed specifically for biscuits, bread, cakes or animal feed. These differing strains of wheat have been developed for food made by machine. At home we have made bread from so-called strong wheat (or strong flour), biscuit flour, animal wheat feed and ordinary plain flour made from a variety of wheat destined for cake making. When you are making bread by hand it hardly matters. You can still make brilliant, tasty and sustaining bread.

The point of this is that the first time I tried to find wheat I could only get animal feed wheat, but I grew it all the same. Doubtless, there are lots of reasons for growing only bread wheat for bread, but I have to confess I didn't notice any difference when I ate animal feed.

Preparing the Ground

You need bare earth. The first thing John Seymour did when he moved to Ireland was to take his rotavator to a field and break it up to grow wheat. My little tiller does well at chopping weeds out, but it is hard work.

If you have land from a previous crop, and potatoes are a good one, then you can dig this over and rake it to make a tilth. You can sow your wheat in April. You broadcast the seed so that the soil is evenly covered and looks as though you have peppered it. Then you rake it in.

You need to have used up about half a 25kg bag per large allotment. A good handful and a half per square metre. On a field scale you are probably better using a seeder. They seem a bit extravagant but there is nothing better. They give a very even spread and at the same time provide a very measured amount of seed. They are not that expensive and if you are doing this every year they are money well spent.

When it first grows it looks just like grass. Agriculturists have names for every stage of the plant's growth, but we needn't worry about any of that. Eventually it heads out and you have the flower on the top of the stalk.

Fine Balance

Wheat grows in proportion to the fertility of the soil. If you have a very rich soil it will grow very quickly. Anyone who has kept a lawn will know that it dries the soil. Imagine a lawn where the grass is nearly a metre tall! In the years I have grown it I have tended to use a plot that had been fertilised for a previous crop. Besides, we tend to over fertilize our allotments anyway. In dry weeks you might need

A major consideration is the fact that individual families have never been self-sufficient. It is more a case of communities being self-sufficient, sharing the grain harvest, and in more recent history, selling it. So important is the grain harvest to the communities of England that there are hundreds of examples of magistrates imprisoning, flogging and fining workers who allowed too many weeds to grow amongst the wheat.

to water the crop.

Harvest

The crop will yellow as it ripens and by late August it is ready for collecting. The grains in the heads ripen and swell. At first they are what is called 'milky ripe' at around six to eight weeks before the harvest is ready. If you thrust your thumb nail into the seeds they will ooze a milky liquid.

The grain is actually ready when it is hard, dried and will rub out of the head in your hands.

I have never swung a scythe. Anyone out there who wouldn't mind teaching me will receive my undying gratitude. You don't have to believe me, but it's true none-the-less. I have cut wheat with secateurs, wallpapering shears, a petrol driven brush clearer, some gardening shears and a very sharp knife. Each method was back breaking, but good training prior to the new rugby season. It takes a long time, so try and do it in a week when the weather is uniformly calm.

If it rains you are as well looking for a break where the crop can dry out again. We do not have dryers, so the crop has to be taken dry. If it rains and rains then fungal infections will start to turn the crop black and this is a dangerous sign.

Collect as much wheat as you can hold in your arms at a time and get it under cover if it is likely to rain, or leave it stood up outside if not. These are the stooks. You can tie these up to make them easier to handle.

The grain is beaten out of the heads. This is called threshing. Some people use a flail, which is simply two stout sticks hinged in the middle with a chain or some leather. Put a large cloth on soil (not concrete because you'll bash a hole in it) and spread the stooks.

I prefer to use the back of a chair to bash the grain out because, as I am still holding the straw, it is easier to put to one side once it is finished. Simply put the chair on the cloth – an old sheet will do – and take all your frustrations out on the chair with the wheat.

Winnowing

I give the grain a good rub to release any sticky chaff and then over the sheet, on a windy day, throw the grain into the air. The wind blows the chaff away. It really excites me that humans have been doing this for nearly ten thousand years.

Storage

Wheat needs to be stored dry, in sacks where any excess moisture can escape. We do not have any special storage tanks, but half full dried agricultural sacks are good enough. Check the wheat from time to time for dryness.

The Urban Farmer

Steps in training an Espalier Tree

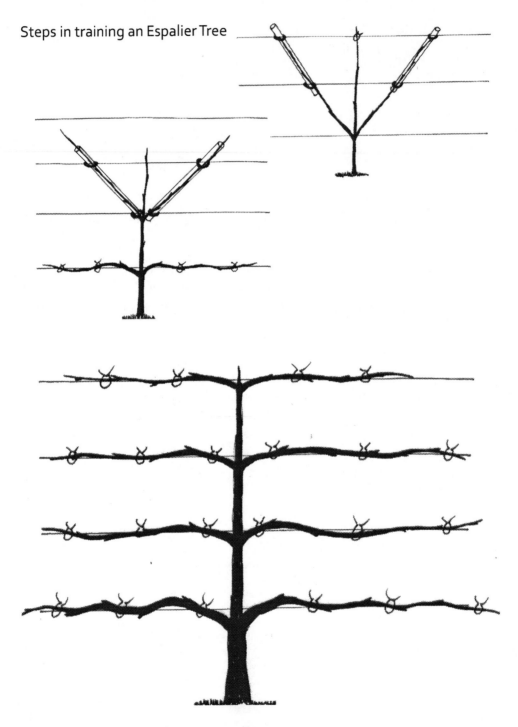

Chapter Nine

The Urban Orchard

Fruit is divided into Top fruit, which is fruit that grows on trees such as apples, pears, cherries, plums, cobs and filberts, walnuts, hazelnuts and quince. The rest are soft fruit, mostly raspberries, gooseberries, currants of various kinds and, although strawberries are pretty soft, often top- and soft-fruit nurseries don't sell or include them in their lists. Both top fruit trees and soft fruit bushes come as bare-rooted plants.

Top fruit

Wouldn't it be wonderful to have your own orchard! If only we had enough room I could plant apples and pears and plums and run pigs beneath them in the traditional way. Unfortunately I don't have the space. But, as you should expect from this book by now, that shouldn't put you off. There are many reasons for growing fruit in the garden.As the old man said on the television advert said when pouring himself a stout, "It looks good, it tastes good and by golly, It does you good!"

Apples, for example, are probably one of the healthiest fruits you can grow and, after the initial hard work of getting a young tree established, they are really easy to keep on, producing a fresh supply of apples year on year. Dreams of keeping pigs in an orchard aside, you do not need a lot of land to grow wonderful apples.

You can grow apples and pears as stand alone trees, training them along wires as cordons or growing them against walls as espaliers. You can prune them to become very thin plants taking up next to no room, you can grow them in containers or even train them into a hedge.

You can find a type of tree that will be right for you, whatever your situation.

Buying fruit trees

Many trees come with roots that are not their own, but have been grafted in position in order to create a certain sized tree. Rootstocks are used because there is no real way of determining the size of a mature tree. MM106 is the main stock used in commercial orchards and, if un-pruned, will give a slender tree about 10-12ft in height. The National Fruit Collection at Brogdale, Kent, is on M9, which reaches about 8ft. Trees on M27 are not much bigger than a tomato plant and after several years of shaping, need no pruning. You can tell a grafted tree because it has a wound where the scion (branch) was fixed to the stock (root). The label should give you all the information you need and these trees should be planted so the wound is at ground level.

If there is one word in horticulture that I can't stand it is dormancy. We're told to do such and such a job on the tree when it is supposed to be dormant, as though it was hibernating while it is too cold to grow. The truth is that deciduous plants, those that lose their leaves in the autumn, are not dormant at all. They are simply saving nutrients and water during the winter, a period when it is too cold to make the process of photosynthesis a profitable exercise.

In fact, all plants are doing something, even the dead ones! Most deciduous trees are growing internally, layers of tissue-producing cells called cambium are busily dividing – producing the wood that will expand in the spring to make the tree bigger.

The real benefit of deciduous trees is that you can do all sorts of things to them and they won't drop dead so long as they have no leaves. As soon as leaves appear, the tree has to be left alone with its roots in moist soil for the rest of the spring and summer. This is because it's the leaves that act as a heart, pulling moisture through the plant from the roots and in turn forcing sugar-rich sap to all the other parts of the plant. Once the leaves are gone, water and food movement slows to a trickle and the plant switches into winter mode.

Bare or Ball?

There is a difference between bare-rooted and ball-rooted trees. The former usually come in a plastic bag which has the tree branches already pruned and bare roots in the bottom – sometimes wrapped in moist newspaper. Ball-rooted plants come with their roots in a net that also houses some compost. These are usually found in garden centres and are more convenient because the balls can be watered and the tree will manage for a year or so quite happily, so long as it doesn't dry out.

On the whole, bare-rooted stock do better than ball-rooted or container grown plants because they have unencumbered root systems that have been allowed to grow normally.

How to Plant Top Fruit Trees

You should get your plants into the soil as soon as they arrive. While it's in the plastic bag the tree is slowly dying and, once the root has dried out, the plant will be dead. If you can't plant it in its final position, simply dig a spit (a slit in the ground) and place it in this. Failing that, keep it in its package in a cool shed.

You need to dig a frighteningly large hole 1m in diameter and 60cm deep. Keep the soil, removing any stones and any roots as you find them. Add to this 30% of the volume of really good, well rotted manure or compost. Also add a good handful of bonemeal or other organic fertiliser (but don't forget to wear gloves!)

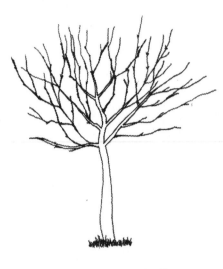

Vigorous young tree before prunning and festooning.

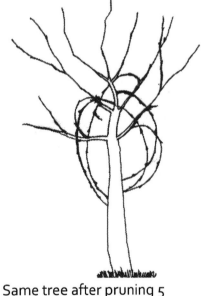

Same tree after pruning 5 shoots forming a festoon.

Improve the drainage of the soil beneath the hole – especially important where clay is involved. Do this by adding stones, digging away with a fork at the soil and, if necessary, digging a channel away from the planting site.

When you are ready to plant, put a tree stake into the centre of the hole and drive it home. People often do this once the tree has been planted and the hole filled, but I always worry about damaging the roots. Line the bottom of the hole with a few spades of the soil mixture and then tie the tree to the stake with a real tree tie with a buckle so you can loosen it off later. Don't use string as it will rub the bark off.

Firmly but carefully fill in the hole, using your feet to compress the soil. Try not to shock the tree by stamping or bashing the earth with the spade – all that energy has to go somewhere and you can easily damage the roots.

Finally, give the tree a long, long drink of water. Try to keep the area around the tree weed-free, and certainly don't allow grass to grow. Young trees have been fatally damaged by gardeners getting too close with the lawn mower!

Top fruit trees need care and rarely produce fruit in the first year. It can be up to three years before you get good quality fruit and these early days are important. Feed the plant with a good quality compost mulch each spring and keep it free from disease wherever possible.

Once the tree has established itself it will go on giving you perfect fruit for a generation to come, so being careful at the start is well rewarded later.

Setting Fruit

Some varieties of apples and pears are self-fertile. Most plums are self-fertile too, but you need to consider pollination. Some plants will need a pollination partner nearby and, when it comes to growing in an urban situation, you can pretty much guarantee this is the case. However, some fruit are very special indeed. The so called triploid fruit have three sets of chromosomes and need two other non-triploid trees to pollinate them. The Bramley is a triploid, which is quite popular.

There is no better way of pollinating top fruit than with bees – you get 30% better pollination around the garden with a beehive than without.

Apples and pears are easy to care for when they are established. Each spring give them a good mulching with well rotted manure and a few handfuls of organic pelleted fertiliser.

Pruning Apples

In year one just reduce the length of the tree by half – there should be only one

You can plant ball-rooted trees at any time of the year so long as you're careful not to damage the roots and you give them plenty of water when you put them in. Bare-rooted trees need to be planted in the winter or early spring at the very latest.

branch. Do this straight after you have planted it. In year two and three and in subsequent years you only prune the new wood in December to February. Reduce its length by a third, cutting with a slant just above an outward facing bud.

Pruning pears is much the same, though they do tend to have a more upright growth, so this will have to be borne in mind when choosing outward facing buds on the new year's growth.

Grapes (The Urban Vineyard?)

A generation ago you would have to be a good gardener indeed if you were to keep a grape vine. Today they are commonplace and easy to grow if you stick to the rules. A polytunnel is probably the ideal place to grow grapes, especially in the cooler north of the country. But now many farmers are successfully growing commercial stock in the UK; mostly all converted into wine of ever increasing quality.

Varieties

Gone are the days when all you could get was Black Hamburg, which gave a lot of smallish, reasonably sweet fruit. There are now a large number of varieties available to the grower and you can not only grow good eating fruit, but also get a good approximation of some of the world's favourite wine grapes.

These varieties are easily available and grown in the UK. You can grow almost any variety under cover, although it is best to choose the late-ripening ones. There are scores more too!

Bacchus
A German white variety that gives excellent juice.

Siegerrebe
A very early maturing variety, bred from Gewurztraminer, producing delicious brownish grapes.

Schonburger
Grown particularly in Kent and a good flavoured grape with lots of sugar.

Mueller-Thurgau
The commonest German grape with a very flowery aroma.

Seyval Blanc
Grown a lot in the USA. A small white fruit, heavy cropping and now used mainly for sparkling wine.

Madeleine Angevine
A citrus flavour, ideal for cool climates which ripens early and a very reliable cropper.

Black Hamburg
The original gardener's grape – fantastic for lots of good fruit, if grown under cover.

Triomphe D'Alsace
Like blackcurrants, with good sweetness and a reliable, slightly foxy flavour.

Pinot Noir
Just to show you can grow one of the classic varieties. Susceptibility to Botrytis is the problem.

Planting

There are a number of traditions about growing grapes indoors. Firstly, the root is planted outside a greenhouse and the vine trained inside through a window. The other tradition is to grow a vine in a hole half filled with a dead sheep but I think we'll pass on that one.

However, the extra space in a polytunnel makes it possible to plant the vines in bush form, as though they were outside in a vineyard. We shall concentrate on the old-fashioned greenhouse method, growing the plant as a cordon outside the tunnel/greenhouse.

Should the necessary dead animal not be available, dig a hole 60cm (2ft) deep and at least twice as wide as the root ball and line the base with manure. Keep the dug soil and mix half of it with an equal amount of compost.

Tease the roots and place them onto the manure, filling in with the soil / compost mix. Firm well, using as much soil as you can fit into the space. Cover the base of the plant with a good layer of compost as mulch.

Initially it will be important to stake the vine (certainly for the first year), allowing it to grow freely and become established. It can be supported inside the tunnel on an end brace or a specially erected pole

Vines create a lot of shade and are best in full sun. Tomatoes do not make good bedfellows with vines because of their height and the evaporation from the tomato leaves creates an atmosphere that tends to promote fungal infections in the sweet grape fruit.

Pruning as a Cordon

Training your vine at a little higher than head height and tied to firm supports will produce a strong vine. You will need to consider erecting something more than just the hoops of the polytunnel, which are usually too far apart to be an effective support. You will need something along the lines of a system of wires at 30cm intervals. Each of these wires will support a lateral, which will bear fruit. The leader, a branch in other words, will run at 90° to these wires.

In the first two years do not allow any fruit to form on the plant. You are simply building the structure and making it strong.

After a year choose your leader branch and tie/support it until it reaches your wires.

Any sub laterals should be plucked out entirely. You are only choosing one leader at this point.

In the winter, collect the fallen leaves and cut the leader back to where it is at least pencil thickness, cutting just after a bud.

Repeat this in the second year, so that now you will have a main stem and two leaders. From the third year on you can train a lateral off each leader. Remember, grapes appear only on new wood, so each year you prune the lateral 'cordon' canes back to about 10 buds (or you can use more short 3-bud spurs).

Problems

Fungal infections come in three forms:

Botrytis occurs in wet conditions and is kept at bay by good pruning.

Downy mildew occurs where the temperature is really hot and the greenhouse or tunnel very humid.

Powdery mildew forms on the leaves and fruit. You can prune it away by cutting out the infected leaves and fruit, keeping the tunnel or greenhouse really clean.

People allow too much fruit to develop and then wonder why they are all covered with botrytis. The keyword is ventilation. Cut out bunches of grapes that fall near each other, leaving plenty of space for air to ventilate and remove humidity. Fungal infections thrive when the humidity and temperature is high.

Mildew and Botrytis are best dealt with using a copper based fungicide. Bordeaux mixture was invented 150 years ago by monks to treat vines in France and was on the organic list for many years. Not now strictly thought of as organic, many gardeners still use it. I can't understand why it was removed from the organic list. It has been used for ages and ages with no measurable effects on the environment at all.

Your alternative is to grow one of the less susceptible varieties and keep the humidity low and the grapes widely spaced – at least no more than 18 bunches

Indoor vines do well if they are fed with tomato fertiliser each month from a couple of weeks after they have burst into life in the spring, until the grapes are ready for picking. Since the bark is fibrous, all kinds of pests over-winter and so scrape some of the bark away inside the tunnel or greenhouse with a nail brush. If you are growing grapes in Scotland then it's a good idea to heat the greenhouse to 4o°C from mid-winter onwards. This will give them a good head start.

to a mature plant.

Keys to Success

- Fruit is produced on one-year-old growth
- The plant will bleed if you cut it in the growing period
- The fruit will rot if the atmosphere is too moist
- Plants like a good feed once a year
- Vines prefer to be cold in the winter

You need to remember that whatever pruning regime you use, you need to have some shoots that, this year, will grow leaves but no fruit, so that next year they can produce fruit. All pruning takes place at the end of the season when the plant isn't actively growing. If your tunnel or greenhouse is heated you are best to grow grapes as standards in large tubs so they can be placed in the cold during the winter.

Harvest

The big problem with grapes, or at least with the fruits, is that they are full of sugar and, unless you have good ventilation between the berries, penicillium fungi will infect the bunches. You can use scissors (some growers have special scissors just for the purpose) to thin out the berries so that the others can grow unencumbered and a good air-flow around the grapes is achieved.

The cardinal rule on harvesting is to cut off the piece of lateral they are growing from so that you do not have to touch the grapes and either contaminate or damage them.

Peach

There are few things more reminiscent of summer than peaches and nectarines and they can be grown, although success can be somewhat patchy, depending on the summer. However, if you grow in the polytunnel or the greenhouse you will almost invariably get good fruit.

Probably one of the best ways of growing them is in pots so you can take them outdoors if the weather is fine.

Varieties and Rootstocks:

Most UK varieties are grown on vigorous rootstocks so they will need heavy pruning.

Bellegarde is a heavy cropper with tasty fruit.

Peregrine gives medium to large crimson red fruit.

Amsden June is a hardy and reliable variety. Probably the best all rounder.

Nectarine varieties:

Elruge is great under cover, but not so good outside.

Humboldt is a heavy cropper.

Care

The plants drop their leaves and it must be cool but consistently frost free. Stand them near the door of the polytunnel. As soon as it warms in the spring make sure the area is well ventilated. The opposite is needed in the height of summer, when they prefer a humid position. So keep the humidity high by spraying the floor and misting the foliage.

Pollination

Once the flowers are open, simply brush them with a soft camel hair brush. Once the fruits are forming, thin them out to around 10-12 per plant at first.

I treat them like tomatoes by feeding with tomato feed each month, usually quite sufficient for normal production. The fruits appear on new wood, so you can prune back the plant following fruiting.

Peach leaf curl, aphids and red spider mite are the major problems and if you grow indoors leaf curl is usually very minor. Peach leaf curl is a fungal problem. You should collect leaves that are swollen and blotchy red and burn them. Spray the plant with Bordeaux mixture – this will keep the plant in reasonable order.

The Urban Farmer

Melons

Strictly speaking the melon *(Cucumis melo)* isn't a fruit. It is is related to the cucumber and the gherkin and is an ancient plant that probably originates in the Far East, but has been cultivated for so long that its true origins are obscure.

The fruits are very versatile and even their skins have been used for millennia. Dried and ground up they are added to wheat flour to make bread and the seeds are the best and most ancient cure for tapeworms.

The melon plant is frost sensitive. It will live through quite harsh frosts but will not then go on to produce any decent fruit. There are four things to bear in mind when it comes to growing melons.

Good rich soil, good drainage, considerable watering with plenty of nutrients – especially phosphates and heat. In Turkey escapee melons from gardens have become a serious problem in the wild where they grow as weeds. Of course the problem we have is a lack of heat, so consequently you will have greater success indoors than outside.

Melon varieties

Banana Melon
The banana melon is like a slim rugby ball, quite ancient and fairly easy to grow indoors.

Cantaloupe Melon
'Hale's Best Jumbo' is a sweet melon well worth cultivating. It is an old variety that has hardly been surpassed for consistent quality.

Israeli Melon
Ogen was a kibbutz where this melon was developed in the 1960s. It can produce a lot of fruit – especially in hot summers.

Rocky Ford Honeydew Melon
This is an American melon – originally green fleshed then orange. A good all rounder and very sweet

Persian Melon

These are small and found all over the Middle East. They ripen on the vine and have deeper roots – so need less watering – than the others. These are very ancient melons that were probably taken around the world.

Growing melons indoors

You need a good soil, rich with well-rotted compost. There is no need to grow melons in a 'hot bed' of fresh manure. Tests have shown that this method simply rots the roots. You can start in April.

Plant two seeds close together by simply pushing them into the compost. The next plant is grown a good arm's length away. Melons are climbers so a good support trellis is a prerequisite. Now all the advice starts to differ. Once the plants have germinated, pinch out the least vigorous one to leave the best for growing.

The usual advice is to nip out the growing point after four leaves have appeared. This produces four side shoots that grow vigorously and produce both male and female flowers. It is said that you should pollinate the females manually by pulling off a male flower and dusting all the insides of the female flowers with it on the same day, so you tend to get the same sized fruit. Well it doesn't work like that in reality.

You can grow the plant out and stop it after ten leaves if you like, or three – you decide. Clearly the more fruits you have

The peach bush needs a rich soil that is well drained. Each year you should give plenty of well rotted manure and dig in lots of organic matter prior to planting. A thick layer of mulch, reapplied each year, will retain moisture. You can decide how to grow your bush, either as a fan, as a cordon on wires or as a bush. Personally I prefer a bush because it gives me plenty of opportunity to move them around.

on the plant, the smaller they will be. For me I like to pinch out flowers once I have three good growing fruits on a plant.

Runaways

You have to remember that plants do not like to reproduce that much. If they are very lush, the numbers of flowers will reduce. They might not even produce any female plants at all. You have to shock them into reproduction mode by cutting down the water, cooling the greenhouse and adding a little shade.

If the melon is on the floor, then protect it with a mat or some straw. You can also protect them by holding them up in little nets. Maintain the watering every couple of days at the roots, with a correctly diluted tomato feed every second watering. If you over water them the melons will taste very watery.

Growing Melons Outside

Most melons are grown on a little volcano like ridge to allow increased drainage, increased warming and sunlight and for the plant to lollop over. The best results are started indoors. Sow two seeds in a small pot of compost in April (March if it is heated) and pinch out the smaller plant, leaving one to grow.

Keep this plant growing until June, when it can then be planted outside. A couple of weeks prior to planting out, make a mound around 40cm high with a little well in the top for the plant. This soil should be rich in well-rotted compost. Cover with black plastic. This allows the soil to heat up in whatever sunlight there is. I tend to keep the plastic in place throughout the cropping period.

When you transplant the melon, try to cover it with a cloche for as long as you can. I have made a little tent in the past from clear plastic that fits over the plant when the weather is poor. Melons need heat and good sunlight.

In the UK, especially in recent years, the temperatures have been quite warm and the only problems are the wind and rain. If you can grow them in a bright but sheltered spot, the local temperature should be good enough to produce a decent crop. Driving wet winds are a killer, though, as they reduce the temperature and promote rot.

I have found that the best results came from watering every third day outside and feeding every second watering. However, in very hot weather this has increased to daily watering. Once the melons are ripening the watering can be restricted. It is best to make sure that the watering is even, with no prolonged periods of drought compensated by huge rivers of water!

Stop the plant to produce side shoots in exactly the same way we have discussed for greenhouse grown plants. Pollinate them by hand as the female flowers appear. Again I keep three good ones rather than a lot of small ones per plant.

Harvesting

All melons, except the Persian or Turkish types, slip off the vine. You move the fruit about and it falls off! You can store these melons and they will tend to get sweeter. The Persian types remain fixed to the vine and you have to cut them off. These types do not change much in storage at all. Persian melons do tend to smell very aromatic when they are ripe, and you should use this as a guide for harvesting.

Problems and diseases

There are a number of problems with melons. The whole family has problems in the UK from the temperature, too much water, late frosts, too little water and over feeding.

As the plant grows its cells have an optimum size. Frost and too much water changes this and the result is a few broken cells, spilling their contents into the tissue of the plant. The plant can cope with a small amount, and it has an immune system designed to mop up these changes. However, if it happens to excess or on repeated occasions then the immune system shuts down and fungal infections take over.

The most common problems are powdery mildew and root rot. Since the fruits are full of sugar they are a prime target. There is little you can do about it except to spray with Bordeaux mixture once a month. By far the best way of keeping the plant in good order is to protect it from extremes of heat, cold and drought. Also avoid anything other than well rotted compost – there is no need to introduce fungi when the plants are susceptible to start with.

Oranges and lemons

All members of the citrus family – oranges, lemons, limes, grapefruits and so on – are prized for their flavoursome fruits and their vitamin C content, but they actually contain no more vitamin C than most other plants.This notion has stuck around since Georgian times, when they were used on long sea voyages to ward off scurvy.

When you think of citrus fruit, oranges and lemons immediately spring to mind. But it's possible to grow much more than this in the UK. Clementines, mandarins, satsumas, grapefruits, kumquats and limes, as well as bergamot – so you can even make your own Earl Grey tea – all do well over here.

Something in Common

All citrus plants can be grown relatively easliy in the UK as long as you make sure you provide a frost-free environment in the winter months. Cold, wind and rain combine to make these plants miserable, meaning they need to be brought inside in the autumn. They are tolerant of cold down to around 5°C, so an unheated polytunnel is best. Try to keep them in the sunniest places, not necessarily for the heat it brings, but because they'll prefer it.

Just because it's winter doesn't mean that citrus plants are going to 'sleep.' In fact, they actively grow during this period, and most of them flower in the winter too. An orange in flower on Christmas day is a lovely thing!

Clearly, if they're to be brought in during the winter, these plants need to be grown in pots. For preference, a large terracotta pot is best because it's porous and provides an amount of air to the roots. In addition it will more readily allow for the evaporation of water, plus store heat for much longer than a plastic equivalent. As far as size is concerned, a 60cm pot for a small citrus tree will be perfectly adequate.

Fill it with a soil-based compost (John Innes No.2) and incorporate some sand into the mix, say up to 25% of the volume. All citrus plants generally need the same regime when it comes to watering and feeding. They don't like to stand in wet conditions, but they do enjoy moisture. However, take care not to over-water; simply make sure that the soil is slightly moist, and that the pots are positively free-draining.

Use a good quality general fertiliser (making certain that it has all the necessary trace elements), at least once a month – possibly once a fortnight in the spring. Some people use a winter feed and a separate summer feed, but as long as you use a good quality, all-round fertiliser, this expense isn't necessary in my view. Feed less in the winter, just once a month or so.

Re-potting and Pruning

This is best done in the spring. Trim your plant just above a fat, lush-looking bud so that the tree takes on a good, roundish shape and remains at the appropriate height for your tunnel.

Re-pot yearly into the next size up. Take the opportunity to add some slow-release fertiliser and fresh, well-draining compost. Gently remove some of the soil and ensure there is plenty of crockery in the bottom of the new pot for drainage. Add some new compost/sand mixture and firm in well. Give a good watering, and keep the plant out of draughts/wind for a few days.

Pests and problems

All members of the citrus family suffer from the same group of pests; aphids, red spider mite and scale insects. A weekly wash with soft soap will keep most of these in check. They drop their leaves regularly in winter, but should not lose more than a third. Any evidence of yellowing leaves could be due to over-watering, lack of nutrients, low temperatures or insufficient sunlight.

Keep plants well ventilated, but out of strong draughts to avoid botrytis and other fungal infections.

Above all, water well but don't allow them to stand in water.

The Urban Farmer

Oranges

Every navel orange is a descendant of a single mutant tree found in the early nineteenth century in Brazil. It was budded and the small plants sent around the world. They're a very heavy fruit and, consequently, the trees need to be large to take their weight. The fruits are seedless and have a small 'baby' fruit inside them.

Blanco oranges are smaller and so can be borne on smaller trees. Most fruits can be harvested from November to December.

Grapefruit

Grapefruit first appeared in the West Indies – again another mutation – in 1750, and were transported as buds all around the world. They were particularly prized by rich English landowners who grew them in hot houses, even though they can be dragged outside in the summer. The plants are larger than orange trees, and bear larger fruits. Otherwise they can be treated in exactly the same way.

Kumquats

This is a fast-growing tree and the fruits can be eaten whole. They are also supposed to be good pickled in brandy. They grow to be quite large and, for this reason, are kept in a single position.

Clementines and satsumas

These plants ripen around Christmas, most being ready after November. They can be kept quite small, even though they are vigorous plants. Annual trimming keeps them in check, but you can grow them up a wall or as a large bush.

Limes and limequats

Limes tend to be easy to grow and can be restricted to a reasonably small tree of about 1.7m in height. There are a number of varieties and each grows well in the UK – some turning yellow when ripening.

A limequat is a cross between a lime and a kumquat. You can eat the whole fruit, and it tastes like a lime.

Citrus savvy!

Whichever citrus plant you want to grow, they're easy as long as you follow the rules:

- Keep plants cool but frost-free in winter – a minimum of 5°C

- Water freely, but ensure good, free-drainage

- Feed regularly in the summer and less in winter

- Prune and re-pot in spring

- Keep the atmosphere humid by watering paths and, if kept inside all year round, ensure good ventilation during hot weather

Blueberries

Blueberries require a well-drained, fertile and acidic soil. If grown in a lime soil, (with a pH of 5.0 and above), blueberries can't absorb iron. This leads to an iron deficiency in the plant, which means they won't grow properly, will produce very little, if any, fruit and could eventually die. Most gardeners feed their acid-loving plants with a sequestered iron liquid feed, or grow them in pots of ericaceous compost.

Blueberries grow well in pots due to their fussy soil requirements, though they

Propagation

Most citrus plants will grow readily from fresh seed, but will take around a decade to flower and fruit, sometimes two. Plants can be grown by taking hardwood cuttings in the autumn; around half will 'take' and, after a couple of years, the trees might produce fruit. All citrus plants bought from garden centres and nurseries are grafted on to specialised rootstocks, and the vigour that this ensures means that they will grow to their full height very quickly.

Most citrus plants are propagated by budding, with a single bud grafted on to a rootstock/scion combination.

should always be fed with rainwater, as tap water contains lime. They enjoy full sun or partial shade and you should grow at least two plants so they cross-fertilise and produce bigger yields.

Plant the bushes in pots at any time of the year and in autumn or spring if you're putting them straight into the ground. Prepare the soil by digging in plenty of rich, organic matter and include chipped bark or sawdust as these usually contain high levels of acid. If the plant has any flower buds or signs of new growth, remove these so it focuses its energy on generating a healthy root system. Place the plant in a hole 50cm deep and wide and firm the soil around the stem gently. Keep them well watered (if you're short on rain water, mix a little vinegar in some tap water and use that as a substitute).

Gooseberries

There's a story told in darkest Lancashire about a market trader who rubbed the hairs off his goosegogs and sold them to unsuspecting mill folk as grapes. They had never seen grapes, so they didn't know any better, but the gooseberries were so sweet they found they preferred them to the real thing once they eventually appeared on the market.

Whether the story is true or not is difficult to say, but the gooseberry is the ideal bush fruit for northern climates. It prefers to mature slowly over a long cool summer. If the weather is hot and bright the fruit matures quickly, but the sugar content takes a while to catch up. They do well on a north facing wall, but if you are north of the Midlands, plant them in full sun, but in the south plant in partial shade.

Gooseberries also do well in poor soil as long as it's well drained. Besides, you can always improve the soil by digging out what you have and putting some new in its place.

Drainage is the Key to Perfect Gooseberries

The time to plant gooseberries is any time from October until late January, if the ground is not waterlogged or frozen. October is probably best because there is still some warmth about and you have the chance of giving your plant a foothold.

Planting

Dig a hole as wide as the widest branches and at least as deep as the roots. They like to be moist but not to stand in water, so add a little grit to the bottom of the hole to improve drainage. Incorporate as much organic material as you can into the soil, ideally well-rotted manure or good quality compost. Firm the plant in well with your heel and give it a mulch of compost on the top.

Always remember that the mulch should never actually touch the stem of the plant – it can rot if the compost gets wet. Plant gooseberries at 1.5m spaces and leave them to bed in.

Feeding

In the spring give them another mulch and in the autumn a handful of some slow-release fertiliser such as bonemeal. This is all they need, except for a plentiful supply of water as long as there is fruit on the boughs, but don't let them stand in wet soil.

Pruning

Gooseberries can be so prolific that they gain a micro-climate of moist air around the fruit and consequently suffer from the fungal attack known as mildew. This is made worse by the thorns that stop the air from circulating, making the whole plant a moisture trap. I wouldn't mind but the birds have long since worked out how to get at the fruit without getting hurt!

Pruning takes place in February. All you're trying to do is to keep the centre of the bush as open as possible to allow the air to circulate. Remove any dead wood and then have a look for any crowded branches. That's all there is to it. You don't have to worry about which branches to take out for fruit production. Just make the plant cup-shaped and open.

Removing fruit

Around May you'll get an idea of how prolific the plant is. Take away some of the small fruit to allow the air to circulate around individual fruits. This also gives them room to grow and ripen without hindrance.

Grow in a pot

To grow gooseberries in a pot you must make sure they won't be standing in water. Buy a good ceramic pot at least 30cm in diameter and fill it with a layer of grit, followed by good quality compost. Each pot will house a single plant which will do well if it's pruned slightly more heavily than normal in February.

Remove some of the compost in spring and replace it with new and every three years put on to a new terracotta or ceramic pot one size larger than before.

Gooseberry Varieties	
Alma	Bright red, a good table variety
Ashton Red	Medium to large, full of flavour, lots of fruit
Australia	Large, early, golden yellow, a good dessert flavour
Broom Girl	Golden, very large, you can win great prizes with this one - or make some fantastic wine
Hinnonmaki Rod	The greatest enemy of gooseberries is mildew and this variety is virtually immune

Pests

Gooseberries do suffer from aphids so you will need to apply your aphid regime to keep them under control. The other major problem is mildew, which we have already mentioned. You can treat this by using a copper-based organic spray.

Another pest is the sawfly, which leaves holes in the leaves. You can destroy them with your fingers and make sure you change the mulch in the spring to take away any over-wintering insects.

Raspberries

The raspberry is one of the oldest fruits grown in the UK. It predates the Roman conquest and has spread itself around the world because it simply tastes wonderful.

We are blessed in this country with a fantastic climate for growing berries. The plants themselves, particularly blackberries and raspberries, have a genetic trick that keeps them on top of changes in their environment; they hybridise very easily. Consequently they are always merging their genes so that any benefits one might have is quickly transferred to others. This is the reason why brambles are so prolific and difficult to remove once established. To the fruit grower this property means there are always new varieties available for the garden.

I was given an old piece of advice. "Raspberries are thirsty plants that like dry feet." They prefer free draining soils that have plenty of moisture available, but they rot if there is any standing water, and this makes them unsuitable for clay soils. They are woodland plants, so shade is not a problem, but they do much better in full sun.

Summer Fruiting Raspberries	Autumn Fruiting Raspberries
Glen Ample	Autumn Bliss
Julie	All Gold
Joan J	Fall Gold
Octavia	

Summer fruiting raspberries are planted in a trench 30cm deep by 50cm wide and as long as you need. The trench is filled with good quality compost and well rotted manure. This can be done any time in the winter.

Along the length of the centre of the trench a set of three wires is placed at heights varying from 60cm (the lowest) to 1.8 metres (the highest). The raspberries are planted at intervals of 45cm and should be well firmed in using your heel. Pile a little more compost over the base of the plant so it is a hand's depth above the surrounding soil. New raspberries, once planted, should be cut down to 20cm from the soil. Without this they never seem to grow vigorously at all. If any fruits appear in the first year, pull them off and allow all the plant's resources to go into making good roots and healthy crowns. (The crown is that complex system of stems below the surface.)

As they grow they will need supporting on the wires.

The Urban Farmer

In the second year feed the plants in the late spring with an organic fertiliser. A good handful of bone meal for every two plants, forked in with a little compost is a good idea. The canes will grow and fruit. In July or once the harvest has been taken, cut the old cane down to 15cm. Any non-fruiting canes should be tied in and allowed to grow.

Autumn fruiting raspberries

These are stand-alone and need no support. You can simply decide where to grow them. Dig a hole at least 60cm round by 30cm deep and fill with good quality compost/manure as for the summer fruiting varieties. Firm them well in with the heel and place them at least 60cm apart. These should be planted from October to March, avoiding the coldest of the weather.

Pruning should take place in February, not right now in the summer as for the summer fruiting varieties. In this case all you do is take all the growth back to 15cm. New growth will provide flowering shoots. They should be fed each spring with a mixture of bone meal and compost as above.

Care of raspberries

This is largely a question of watering. The fruit, though flavoursome, is largely water and this has to be readily available. They are susceptible to rot, so make sure they drain easily. In dry periods give them a really good soaking once a week. If you live in a drought area, sink some tubing into the soil near the roots when you plant them and water down this tube.

Diseases

Birds will decimate your crop given the chance. The only way I have found to deter them, short of dancing around all day and waving my arms about, is to cover the fruit with net. A fruit cage is the ultimate, and those of you who are really serious about your fruit will want one.

Aphids are a continual pest and your best methods need to be constantly applied to keep them at bay.

The raspberry beetle lays its eggs in very young fruit and the grubs eat the berry from the inside. They eat their way out of the fruit, which becomes misshapen and shrivelled, and the young adults fall onto the ground. You can control this pest with pyrethrum based organic insecticides.

In May it is a good idea to spray the plants with Bordeaux mixture to keep fungal diseases at bay.

All varieties of raspberries, or Rubus Genera, have really interesting genetics. They have hybridised all over the world to produce some really unusual fruits, and Loganberries are just one of them. They have evolved quickly by using a technique unique to plants which is called a change in ploidy. All this means is that they can double or triple the numbers of chromosomes in their cells to create a plant with different characteristics.

Other Berries

To illustrate the various different types of berry you can get we shall have a look at the Loganberry. It is a cross of two other rubus plants, which gives it unusual genetic characteristics. When you buy loganberries you are always guaranteed strong, virile plants with great fruit, but you can't tell if the plants will be fertile and create viable seed.

The Loganberry - A Bit of History

In the 1880s an American Judge, James Harvey Logan, is said to have planted some Red Antwerp raspberries and the American blackberry near to each other and the seeds that resulted had the qualities of both. He didn't cross them on purpose, but this was certainly a period when gardeners were experimenting with hybrids and literally hundreds of crosses of different types of raspberry were created – even the President of the USA produced his own crosses.

Prepare the Soil

Dig a trench or a circle in which you incorporate a good deal of well-rotted manure and compost. They are woodland plants and they like a good nitrogenous soil with plenty of organic matter. The plants fruit on last year's growth so the more you can encourage them to make as much cane as possible, the more fruit you'll have next season.

You can train the loganberry in a wigwam or on a trellis. Over the years the original stock have become less vigorous, but new strains will produce canes up to six feet tall.

Plant them at 45cm intervals and make sure you tie them in. They won't fruit in the first year but the following year you will have fruiting canes and new canes for the following year. You can train them apart from each other. Once harvested you can cut the old canes back to ground level in the winter.

Each year swap over from fruiting canes tied in one place to non-fruiting ones tied in another. The year should run as follows:

Pruning   In the winter, recently flowered canes

Flowering   May onwards

Fruit   Ripe from July, August

Feeding

Give the plants a good feed in the spring. They will be very hungry and you are trying to grow lots of cane, so feed them up with well-rotted manure and, during the summer, give them a feed of organic fertiliser once a month.

Propagation

They will be really vigorous for 10 years, but you can also make new plants from the canes that you cut off by potting them in moist compost and keeping them warm in the polytunnel.

Pests

The main pests will be aphids, leaf hoppers and raspberry beetles. You can easily control these with an organic insecticide. If you simply leave them, which is tempting in the first year, the numbers will undoubtedly build up the following year, resulting in problems.

Blackberries

Blackberries will grow almost anywhere and are often found colonising vast areas of uncultivated land. Choose a sunny site and dig in plenty of rich, organic matter and remove any perennial weed roots that will compete with your crop if left to grow. Buy your plants from a respected nursery and ensure that they are disease-free. Plant them in early spring in moist, well-prepared soil, about 1.5m apart. Cut the plants down to a height of just 15cm and water them well. Apply an organic mulch such as compost or well-rotted manure and top-dress each spring with well-rotted animal manure.

Strawberries

Strawberries are the most strange plants. They are small and delicate looking, but they are actually as tough as old boots. You wouldn't think this weed-like plant would produce so much wonderful fruit, yet it surprises us every year with its abundance. With good management you can have fruit from the early summer right through to autumn. They respond well to all sorts of soil conditions and there are so many hundreds of varieties that there are plenty of opportunities to get some fantastic fruit.

Strawberries get their name from the fact they were traditionally grown with straw under the leaves so that the fruit would not rest on the soil and become spoiled by the mud. The straw also makes for an excellent deterrent against slugs and snails. They're also grown in pots for the same reason, with the fruit dangling over the side or resting on pebbles. You can also use strawberry mats, which are a bit like plastic beer mats, only bigger. A strawberry mat is a brilliant way of controlling molluscs.

Soil and Position

Strawberries are best grown in a sunny position with good drainage. They're very hardy plants and will easily last out a winter with few problems, but new growth in the spring seems to be more susceptible to frost. You should mix in a lot of grit to keep the water at bay as it's

The Urban Farmer

easier to add water to a well-draining soil than to drain it away from a waterlogged soil.

If it's a frosty spring, cover the plants with a cloche, or even a piece of bubble wrap, as young flowers in particular seem to be vulnerable. Another way of avoiding frost damage is to plant them in the highest point in the garden as cold always flows downhill.

Planting

Strawberries are usually sold as new plants and perhaps the very best time to plant them is April and May. This gives them a good growing period before having to face a winter, but plantings in September also do well.

However, you can start them off indoors in the winter – most nurseries certainly sell plants in winter and they can be given a good start in a small pot of compost. Be careful, though. I have frequently had strawberry plants posted to me wrapped in wet newspaper and then pushed into a plastic bag – all mangled up. You never get this problem if you visit the nursery to buy your plants.

Dig the soil to a spade's depth and incorporate a good deal of well-rotted compost. A good handful of grit in the bottom increases the drainage and prolongs the summertime growth if it's rainy. Then, in May, lay straw under the leaves and developing fruit so that none of them are resting on the ground.

Because strawberries are shallow rooted, if you plant them high (that is, to leave a lot of stem showing) they hardly get going at all, and certainly the root systems never become secure. Conversely, the growing point shouldn't be covered with soil at all because it tends to rot. Make sure the plants sit well, but not too deeply.

The plants need to be watered every couple of days when first planted, but after a couple of weeks they should be fine. Don't water so much as to cause puddles. Once established, the plants will start to reproduce, by both flowers and runners.

Runners

Most strawberries throw out sideways branches called runners, and

Strawberries can suffer from fungal problems such as botrytis and mildew, and the best ways of dealing with both of these is either spacing so that air can circulate around them, or copper-based sprays, or both. Some people opt to grow their plants on the top of a little mound, and certainly a well-draining soil will also help to counter these problems.

at intervals little plantlets appear. In the first year these should be cut off to allow the plants to develop. Don't expect the plants to crop much in their first year, but by year two they should be very prolific.

The runners in the second year can be used to create new plants. Where a plantlet appears, simply lift the runner and lay the plantlet into a pot of compost. Anchor this down with a pebble. By the end of the summer you will have another strawberry plant.

Problems

By the third year you plants will probably start to succumb to various viral diseases and will fare less well. You will need a system of removing three year old plants and replacing them withsome of your runner-grown new ones. You should consider replacing about a third of your stock each year. You can also introduce new vigour to your strawberries by buying in completely new stock for about a tenth of your replacement plants.

Your replacement plants can be kept in a cool greenhouse in their little pots over the winter and planted out in March. You will need to acclimatise them to the outdoor life by taking them out during the day and bringing them in at night. These plants are so tough that you can ignore them and they will still grow, even though they may at times look half-dead.

Aphids and red spider mite can also pose a problem but these can be dealt with using any number of organic measures, from the finger and thumb method to organic sprays and biological control.

Strawberry Varieties	
Honeoye	This variety seems to do well in cold, damp situations and has been found to perform well in Scotland
Hapil	Prefers dry conditions and can be susceptible to wilt - but crops really well and the fruits are consistant in size and form
Pegasus	This one is fine in wet conditions and stands up to wilts of all kinds really well too
Cambridge Favourite	This is an old variety that is still going strong. It is disease resistant and gives consistently good fruit
Florence	This one is good on organic plots because it's got a high resistance to disease
Sophie	This crops until late September in warm places
Gariguette	This French variety is unsurpassed for flavour and deserves to be a 'must have' in anyone's plot

Pineapple

This is a bit of fun rather than a practical growing project but is certainly something to talk about if served up! Some supermarkets pull out the growing point of the plant, thus increasing its shelf life. However, no amount of potting and watering will make these crowns grow. Choose a plant that is completely intact. Of course, make sure the fruit is edible because we do not need this part for the growing process, so you might as well enjoy it.

Removing the crown

Some people slice the top with a little flesh beneath; others just twist the crown so it comes away in the hand. Either method is fine so long as there is no flesh attached to the leafy part of the plant.

Once this is done, carefully remove the lower leaves to expose the rootlets, which look a little like a maggot infestation. The tops should be left upright for a week to dry a little. Pineapples are susceptible to fungal infections and if you allow the leaves to get too wet it will undoubtedly rot. Should it show any signs of rot, simply discard and burn it.

Rooting

The embryonic roots need to be tempted into life. This can be done by soaking them for a week in water, being careful not to soak the whole plant, then planting the base of the pineapple into a 20cm (8in) pot filled with good quality compost. Water the compost so it remains slightly moist but not wet. This stage might take several months, but eventually the plant will resist your pulling at it, indicating a root growth.

Dead leaves

The outer leaves will die off, and should be removed. This is a natural part of the growth of the plant and if you look carefully you will see their replacements in the centre.

After a year the plant will need to be repotted into a 25cm pot and it will grow to around 60cm in the next year.

Care

Water your plant sparingly so that the compost is only lightly damp and feed with an all-purpose fertiliser once a month during the summer,. Keep it free from frost at all times, but you can take it outdoors in the summer. A minimum night time temperature of 13°C must be maintained.

Flowering

At around two years old the plant will flower and six months later you will have a small fruit. You can initiate flowering by using the plant hormone ethylene. This is released by bruised apples and other ripe fruit, which need to be in close proximity to the plant.

It will take around six months for your pineapple to grow to a reasonable size and it is ready when the outer shell is golden.

The Urban Farmer

Chapter Ten

Making the most of your Produce

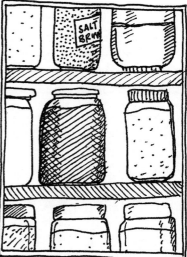

So, you've got your pigs, your chickens and your vegetable patch, not to mention bees, sheep and the family cow.

You will not be able to achieve complete self-sufficiency but that is not the aim of this book. What you will be able to do is to supplement your weekly shop with your own home-produced food.

Your vegetable harvest will provide fresh greens throughout the year, and the glut can be preserved as pickles, jams and jellies.

Your chickens will provide a regular supply of eggs, hopefully, and, if you feel up to it, some will be despatched for the table.

Your cow or goat will provide milk for dairy produce, whilst your pig will give enough meat to keep you in bacon and sausages.

The bees will provide honey and the wheat, bread...I think you get the picture.

Now this chapter could not possibly cover all the various ways of storing, preserving and preparing your produce, but it does cover a few essentials to get you started

Storage

What is essential is to maximise your produce so that you and your family can enjoy it throughout the year. You must give a lot of thought, therefore, to storage and you must definitely plan ahead.

Jars - you can never have too many of these, but give thought to where you are going to store them, both empty and full! Have you a cool, dark and dry place to hang your onions, garlic and dried sausage? Is your freezer really big enough to hold a butchered pig? Do you have the skills and knowledge to make a potato clamp? Have you the energy, as well as the time, to spend hours making jams, chutneys and other preserves?

The Larder

Storage of food that you have harvested is a difficult task for one simple reason. Modern houses are designed simply as a place to sleep and watch the telly. They are certainly not designed for storing a large amount of food for the best part of a year.

This has been the case since Georgian times. Cottage workers, forced into mill working and the first ever urban lifestyle, were fed by giving them tokens to buy food from the mill shop and, hand in hand with the banks, local currencies came into existence. The people's homes were little more than sleeping places. As the nation's industrial base built up, it was considered that because individual workers' houses were the cheapest way of keeping a workforce together, it was justifiable to simply copy the form. Thick stone walled farmhouses and farmworkers' cottages with large larders and great stone shelves simply ceased to be built after the middle of the nineteenth century.

Workforce housing, what we would now call social housing, improved in the twentieth century. In inner city areas the drains, which were often falling to pieces, made it necessary to renew the housing that covered them above ground in order to renew the infrastructure. Houses built in the first half of the twentieth century often contained a small larder, but it was usually far too small to store considerable amounts of food for long periods.

Then, with the rise of the supermarket, housing took a downturn. Today we live in modern versions of the Georgian hovels, with kitchens suitable for little other than warming food in a microwave. How can the government imagine people could possible live healthy lives when the very homes we are supposed to live in force us to eat food pulled from a shelf rather than from the field, allotment or garden?

Building a larder

First of all, larders should be rain and vermin proof, full of air and dry from beneath. They should have lots of shelves and the temperature should be cool without freezing in winter and not hot in the summer. For these reasons your larder should never be a shed which will get too hot, will inevitably leak and will be inundated with mice, rats and all the neighbourhood cats.

The modern answer to temperature fluctuation is insulation, but this is not good enough for a larder – it has to be a substantial building with thick walls capable of absorbing heat. This brings problems in itself. In order to build a structure with thick walls you need substantial foundations and this often requires planning permission and building regulations. I once got around this problem by building a 'room' inside a concrete garage. I built a thick level concrete floor and on top of this I built up concrete block walls inside the concrete walls of the garage. The neighbours wondered if I was building a fallout shelter. The room was two thirds the length of the garage and had a concrete wall with a heavy duty door in it. I laid wooden beams over the top of the room and fitted old floorboards on top to make a roof. On top of the roof I stored hay for the chickens.

Inside I made some shelving using concrete blocks and slate so that the food could be laid on cold rock. I also filled the centre space with wooden shelves. The previous year I had stored my vegetables in a shed. I had gathered two tonnes of potatoes into an old bath and they were rotten within a month. The shed was unbearably hot, but the 'room' was fairly cool in the summer and a bit cooler in the winter. It was a great place to store bottles of beer and wine, but it was too cool for winter brewing.

Drying

The basic idea behind drying food is the same as in most preservation processes; the removal of water. Since the invention of fire, food has always been dried, but the method is not always that easy to judge. Thick pieces of meat might well be dried for preservation on the outside, but some way inside the temperature and conditions might be ideal for bacterial growth.

It is for precisely this reason that a combination of processes have evolved. Drying only thin sheets of material will ensure that the food is uniformly dehydrated and this is a very common and ancient process. Drying associated with salting is also common, particularly for wet, sweet material such as pork and fish.

These processes significantly change the food from its fresh original state, with changes in both consistency and flavour creating an entirely different product. This change is further enhanced by the addition of spices and herbs. Dried beef is no longer beef, dried pork now becomes ham and so on.

The simplest drying methods require fire, and I have no doubt that this led directly to smoking as a methodology. These days we can dry in our kitchens, as they have done in farmhouses for centuries, or in special drying chambers. You can buy desiccators that force the water out of food, or you can maintain a humidity controlled environment in almost any cabinet.

It should be pointed out that all foods can be dried; seeds, beans, peas, corn, fruit, tomatoes etc. Indeed, almost anything. A simple dryer made from plastic can be used in the summertime. It has clear plastic on the sunny side, black plastic on the other and a good plastic floor. The energy from the sun causes evaporation and the food dries out fairly quickly. You simply cannot beat homemade sun dried tomatoes!

Build Your Own Smoker Using a Dustbin

Removing the floor of a new galvanised metal dustbin is no mean feat, but putting enough holes in it to allow the smoke access is a little easier. A fire pit smoker can be made very easily. Simply sink a metal box (a metal bread bin would be ideal) into the earth and start a fire in it. Cover the fire with sawdust to make it smoke.

Place the laden dustbin (laden with your food, that is) over the smoking fire and leave the lid slightly ajar for ventilation. You have to watch this because if the fire becomes too hot, the food will cook. With practise you can gauge the size of fire needed to produce just enough smoke.

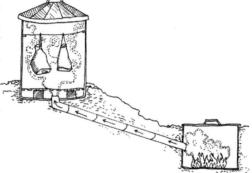

An extension of this method is to punch only one hole in the dustbin and deliver the smoke using a drainpipe as in the illustration.

Making Low Salt Bacon

Choose 500g of pork of any cut you prefer. Loin makes good bacon, but I prefer belly for a very special reason; the salt is only absorbed in the meat, so you only need add it to the meaty bits. Slice it very, very thinly into 20 or so slices. If bought your butcher might be helpful with this

Place it on a tray. Weigh out 7.5g of salt (one and a half level teaspoons) and lightly sprinkle this over all the meat. An alternative way of doing this is to evenly spread half the salt in a roasting tin or a large tray and to simply lay the meat on it, sprinkling the rest of the salt over the top. Cover it with cling film and leave it for 24 hours in the refrigerator. As 7.5g spread over 500g of meat is only 1.5%, the salt content is actually much lower than usual.

Once this has settled, remove the cling film and pour off any liquor that has formed. It is unlikely there will be much. Give each piece a rub to ensure the salt is worked in and then you can add a secondary flavour. I like sugar, honey or smoke or even a combination. Simply sprinkle the bacon with a very light dusting of sugar and leave it overnight. Alternatively, drizzle it with honey and hot smoke.

This product will not last long, not least because it is delicious and usually eaten very quickly. A very large portion contains around 1.5g of salt and the flavour is very good. There is no need to add any saltpetre because the product is only intended to last a few days at most. It can also be frozen.

Basic Sausage Making

This recipe for a simple pork sausage has nothing else in it other than salt, pepper, water, a little cereal and pork, of course.

You Will Need	
1kg of pork shoulder	1 mixing bowl
200g sausage making rusk, or breadcrumbs if you prefer	1 grinder or food processor
	1 sausage stuffer
200ml water	1.25m Hog sausage casing.
1 tsp salt	1 tray to collect the filling sausage
½ tsp pepper	1 knife to cut the links

Open your packet of skins (never mind the smell) and place them in a bowl of clean water. Replace the water several times until the smell goes away. Now rinse the skins under running water, both inside and out.

Chop your meat into centimetre cubes and then grind them. You can also add your other ingredients to this mix. Mix it all together thoroughly. Once you have created your sausage mix you are ready to stuff your casing. Fry a small amount to check that you are happy with the seasoning. If you are then find the end of your rinsed casing

Moisten the delivery tube or nozzle of your stuffer and carefully push the casing on. Leave the end of the intestine open so that, as you force the meat mixture through, the air will escape. Once meat replaces air the skin will be pulled off the nozzle and into a collecting tray.

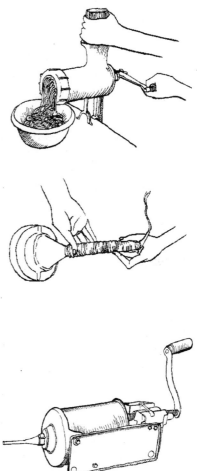

Starting to stuff the casings can be a daunting task, but it is actually quite simple. You will benefit from an extra pair of hands; one to crank the machine (or start it working if it is electrical) and another to manage the flow of sausage from the other end.

Make sure the stuffer is attached very securely to the work surface or wherever you have opted to produce you sausages. A larger capacity mechanical machine can require quite an effort to force the mixture down the nozzle and this effort can occasionally dislodge a less than secure machine.

You can control the thickness of the sausage by gently holding back the casing as it fills with mixture; this will allow more meat per centimetre of sausage, and consequently you will get a thicker sausage.

Don't worry about breakages in the skin. It is bound to happen sometime in your career. Instead, concentrate on maintaining a rhythm and an evenly filled sausage. The first few centimetres might be a little thinner than the rest. For your first try just let the meat take the casing without restriction. Do not over fill it. You will need to leave at least a little room in order to twist your links.

If there are any air bubbles in the sausage you can prick them. Otherwise the casings will burst in the pan. You do not need to be microscopic in your inspection and only larger air spaces need be dealt with. Alternatively, any large bubbles can be cleverly incorporated into the twist links.

If you can, leave the sausages overnight which will improve their flavour, and then cook them. Aficionados call this 'allowing the sausage to bloom.' I haven't managed this step yet. There is always a hot frying pan ready to receive the first few links.

Finally, clean down your equipment straight away, sterilising it all with boiling water if possible. This will make the next batch of sausages easier, though you will have to re-sterilise prior to each session.

Making a basic soft cheese

This cheese can be prepared without a starter, but it is also good with a pot of crème fraiche added to it. The recipe and method are included simply to encourage you to experiment with making some cheese and, for the moment, should be seen as nothing more than that. It is hopefully the magic of the basic process which will encourage you to experiment further in your own time.

You Will Need	
1 gallon (4.5 litres) of milk	a sterile bowl to collect the curds
*4 drops of rennet	a sterile knife
salt	several sterile muslin sheets (cheesecloths)
	a sterile stockpot
* Read the instructions to find out how your own rennet will coagulate in a gallon of milk – use too much rennet and you will end up with a product with the density of concrete but use too little and you will have nothing more than liquid rennet.	

Put the milk into the stockpot either without a starter or with a small tub of crème fraiche or some mesophilic starter. By trying it with and without you will find out how the different components can alter the flavour of your cheese. Then leave it for 30 minutes.

Add rennet – usually one drop per litre of milk. Let the label guide you! A gallon or 4.5 litres looks like a lot of milk but rennet is an enzyme and when the molecule has done its job it is simply released to do its job on the next bit of protein, so a little goes a long, long way. Rennet is dissolved in a small amount of boiled, cooled water. Now heat the milk to 30°C.

Remove the milk from the heat and leave it to set. You will be able to feel the surface of the milk setting like a jelly. This is almost a junket – a sweet made from milk, cream, sugar and brandy.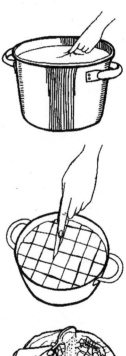

It you thrust your (clean) finger into the curd it should break around it and create a small crack. In other words, in addition to your finger in the mould there should also be a crack around it.

When the cheese has set, cut the curds with a knife. Do this firstly in a criss-cross fashion to make small cubes. You will notice the whey fall out of the curds and, if you sprinkle a teaspoon of salt over them, you will see even more whey come out.

Pour the curds into a colander and wash them under gently running cold water, cutting all the time. The important thing is to get as much whey out as you can.

Gather the curds into a muslin and sprinkle them with 5g of salt and then combine them. You can taste the cheese to see if it is salty enough for you. You will have getting on for 400g of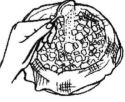
cheese from this so, as it is not going to last forever, you really do not need to over salt it. Next hang the cheesecloth on a hook and allow it to drain overnight.

Now the fun starts.

You can put the cheesecloth of what is now cottage cheese into a mould and put a heavy weight on it to make a harder cake of cheese or you can just smear it over fresh bread and lavish yourself with the joy of having made your first cheese. The basic cheese that you have just made is a brilliant base for:

Chives chopped up small and mixed in with the cheese, then spooned into a ramekin.

Basil finely chopped.

Garlic finely chopped. In fact, if you smear the cheese onto a piece of cling film once you have added your garlic, then coat the top surface with sesame seeds and roll the cheese, you will have an ideal version of a famous French novelty cheese.

Olives: spoon this cheese into the cavity of pitted olives.

Sun dried tomatoes: seriously the most amazing thing you have ever tasted!

You can also use it in recipes for pasta, in fondues and on pizzas or even add sugar and less salt and use it in sweets. You can eat it neat on crackers too, or with your fingers!

Making Jam

Choose fruit that is as fresh as possible. Firm, just ripe fruit is the best, but small amounts of slightly under-ripe fruit may also be used.

The fruit must be washed thoroughly. Hull strawberries, raspberries and any other soft fruit, top and tail gooseberries, currants and elderberries and peel and core apples and pears and any stoned fruit such as plums and apricots.

After washing and preparing the fruit, place it in a pan to pre-cook. This softens the fruit and gets the juices running and the pectin flowing. Sometimes a small amount of extra water may be needed, depending on the fruit.

Bring the fruit slowly to the boil, then simmer until it is tender. Try not to stir the fruit too much as this tends to break it too soon and you will therefore lose some of the flavour of the finished product. The acid content of the fruit is also released in this first cooking time and this helps the pectin to set the jam. If you are using fruits low in acid this would be the stage at which you would add acid, usually in the form of lemon juice.

Fruits with low acid content include strawberries, raspberries, late picked blackberries, cherries, dessert apples, bilberries, peaches, pears and quinces.

Pectin is the setting or gelling agent found naturally in varying degrees in fruit and vegetables. Without pectin jams and preserves would never set sufficiently. It is found in the cell walls and is broken down by heating.

The pectin reacts with the sugar to gel the juices and set. It requires the presence of acid to gel properly, hence the occasional need for lemon juice. If a fruit is naturally low in pectin you can add some. This is either through a home-made pectin stock or by buying a sachet of dried pectin. Specialist sugars may also contain additional pectin. This will be made clear on the instructions.

Some fruit has a medium pectin content and so may require just a small addition. Fruits high in pectin will not need any adding. These fruits are often good to team up with fruits with a low pectin content. If needed pectin is added before the addition of sugar, after cooking the fruit.

Commercially produced pectin is usually sold in powdered form in single sachets. It is essential that you follow the manufacturers instructions for the amounts used. Each sachet of the make I use is designed for use with 1kg of sugar.

Sugar that already contains pectin is useful for very low pectin content fruits.

A Basic Raspberry Jam	
2kg / 4lb raspberries 2kg / 4lb sugar Juice of 1 lemon	Place the fruit in your pan and simmer gently for about 10 minutes until the fruit is soft and the juice is running. Remove from the heat and add the lemon juice. Stir in the sugar and place on a low heat. Stir gently but constantly until the sugar is completely dissolved. Turn up the heat and bring to the boil. Cook at boiling for 4 minutes, checking for setting after this time. When the setting point is reached, remove from the heat, cool for 2 or 3 minutes, stir to distribute the fruit evenly and pour into sterile pots and seal. This should keep for up to 9 months unopened.

A Basic Strawberry Jam	
2kg / 4lb strawberries 2kg / 4lb sugar 2 x 13g sachets pectin or 250ml / 8fl oz pectin stock Juice of 1 lemon	Place the prepared fruit in a pan and heat slowly. Crush the fruit with a masher and add the lemon juice. Heat to simmering and cook for 3-4 minutes until the juices run freely. Lower the heat slightly and add the sugar and pectin, stirring until all the sugar has dissolved. Bring to a rapid boil and cook as such for 4-5 minutes. Test for the setting point and, when ready, ladle into jars.

Chutneys

Chutneys are an excellent way of preserving both fruit and vegetables as they have the longest shelf life of all preserves. So long as all the jars are clean and have an excellent seal they can last for at least 1½ - 2 years. A chutney has a smooth texture and is usually made from finely chopped fruit and vegetables and an individual balance of spices and other flavourings, so that each recipe will be different. They are cooked for quite a long period of time, so the flavours are at their best when left to mature for several weeks before use. Any pungent, spicy flavour will mellow over time and the flavours balance and blend, so don't be tempted to try out your chutney too early as the taste will change for the better over time.

Steps in making chutney.

Step 1 - Preparing the fruit and vegetables

Wash everything well and remove the peel, cores and stalks. Chop everything very finely. A food processor is ideal for speeding up this stage.

Step 2 - Cooking the ingredients

Some, such as blackberries, may need some pre-cooking as they will need to be sieved to remove the seeds. Usually all the ingredients are cooked together, though. The texture of a finished chutney should be both thick and moist.

Step 3 - Potting

Chutneys are put into the jars whilst still hot and sealed immediately. This produces a good seal that allows the preserve to be kept for a long period of time. Once sealed, leave it in the same place until cool, then store it in a cool, dark and dry place.

None of the following chutney recipes are mind -blowingly hot, or over pungent, so they should appeal to most chutney lovers. If, however, you want a more pungent flavour, the amounts of the hotter spices, like chilli or ginger, can be increased. It is advisable to make a trial batch first so that you can make sure it is edible. You may

The Urban Farmer

use spiced or un-spiced vinegar, that is up to you. Spiced vinegar will give a full flavour. It is difficult to give a yield for chutneys as it depends on the type and ripeness of the produce used, so the yield will always be approximate.

Autumn Fruit Chutney	
1.5kg / 3lb mixture of apples, pears, damsons and plums, all cored or stoned and chopped finely	Put all the ingredients into the pan and heat them slowly until all the sugar has dissolved. Stir constantly.
90g / 3oz stoned dates, chopped	Bring it to the boil, then turn down the heat and simmer for 1 hour until the mixture has thickened but is still moist.
90g / 3oz raisins	
450g / 1lb onions, chopped finely	
2 garlic cloves, crushed	Stir and pot it immediately.
230g / 8oz soft brown sugar	Allow it to mature for 2 weeks before using.
1 teaspoon allspice	
1 teaspoon ground ginger	
1 teaspoon ground white pepper	
580ml / 1pint malt vinegar	
1 teaspoon salt	

Apple Juice

To make apple juice you don't really need much equipment. The most important single requirement is a food processor, without which it is very difficult to break the apples up sufficiently to extract the juice.

You can buy presses, but a press will probably not be strong enough to break up the apple on its own and force the juice out. The apple must be chopped up first.

The necessary steps to successful apple juice production are simple enough:

Cut the apples into pieces. Don't worry about the pips or the stalks. Feed them into the food processor and then blast away until the apples are no more than small chips. There is a lot of juice waiting to come out and you will need to fill your press carefully if you are not to lose a lot of it.

Fill the basket of your press. Large presses for fruit that are made from wooden slats need to have the apple chips wrapped in muslin or else you will lose material out of the sides. When you turn the key on the plunger the apple juice is forced out. You can filter this through muslin if you like, but I prefer to have my juice unfiltered. I do, however, pour it through a tea strainer to remove any larger pieces of fruit.

The process is then repeated until you have used up all your apples. The juice will freeze and lasts a long time. I add a little lemon juice, just a tablespoon per litre (a tsp per pint), which stabilises the liquid and enhances the flavour even more.

You can treat pears in exactly the same way as apples, but the juice doesn't last as long. Pears are full of wooden cells called sclerids, which is why they are often used as facial scrubs. You certainly will need to filter pear juice through muslin and must freeze it if you are to keep it for any length of time.

Soft fruit must be washed and wrapped in muslin before pressing, but it frequently mushes to excess and the yield is consequently often low. You are much better making raspberry and strawberry juice by simply boiling the fruit first and then pressing out the juice.

Dandelion Beer

This is based on a recipe that is many centuries old. It originally called for malted barley and dandelions as a flavouring but, to save all the boiling, and most people probably do not have enough space or equipment anyway, we are going to use the blandest beer kit there is. And what could be blander than lager, in my opinion?

The beer kit is little more than wort in a tin. You can get organic beer kits if you like. Most of them contain no preservatives or nasty chemicals, just beer juice. You simply add boiling water to dissolve the thick liquid and top it up to 25 litres (or 43 pints) with cold water. Somewhere in this process you also add a kilo of sugar as a food source, and finally the yeast itself.

If you add sucrose or ordinary packet sugar in any of its varied guises, you will get a funny flavoured beer. This is because glucose is a disaccharide (or double sugar), and when the yeast breaks it down you get the added bonus of a mixture of flavours. Buy glucose from the chemist in the same quantity – usually 1kg (2lbs approx.). You will then get a beer that tastes like pub-bought beer, only better.

In order to add the old, traditional flavour to the beer we are going to add a couple of litres of boiling dandelion water. Since lager is blandish (in fact the nearest beer there is to tea you can get - again, in my opinion), the dandelion will add an interesting flavour, closer to golden bitter than anything else.

Follow the recipe on the can, but the first boiling water should be made by collecting 2 very large handfuls of dandelion leaves boiled for ten minutes in the water. This is then strained into the fermentation vessel. The wort is added, then the sugar (don't forget, you're using glucose!), the rest of the water and the yeast, and away you go!

A Word about Wood: The Ideal Fuel

Wood is perhaps the greatest single resource in the world.

As I write this I am looking through my dining room and living room onto an industrial scene. We live on a fairly small road, though the cars seem to fly down it at an annoying speed, and on the other side of the street is a factory. Beyond, a railway line separates our house from a few million gallons of vinegar, and between the two are around a million pallets crashed over in a haphazard way; ugly but inviting. There is enough wood there to keep our whole estate in energy for the year. They build up into a small mountain and then someone complains about them being a fire risk, and they get someone to take them away. It takes about two months for the factory to build them up again, and so it goes. I followed the man who took them away to see if I could get some only to find that he burned them. He was paid to dispose of them and that's all he did. What a terrible and immoral waste.

Wood is as efficient a fuel as can be and is carbon neutral because, as we all know, the carbon that is released in the burning process came from the atmosphere in the first place. The big problem for urban use is the smoke - we now mostly live in smokeless zones. Smoke, however, is only released by inefficient burning. This is the problem when you burn coal; its impurities come out in the smoke.

When wood burns the first thing to light is the volatile oils in the wood. They are released by the action of heat, but then the wood itself burns. This releases carbon monoxide and various other gasses that would simply disappear up the chimney in a conventional fire. But then the most efficient wood burning stoves pass these gasses into the flames a second time, along with the smoke, and they are burned in the hottest part of the flame. This not only strangles the last drop of energy out of the wood, but makes the exhaust acceptable for town use - even in smokeless zones.

These woodburners are not cheap, costing around a thousand pounds, but usually you can run central heating off them too, which makes them a reasonable bet for house heating - assuming you have

The Urban Farmer

a chimney or a flue. And unless you are an expert, you are best getting one installed professionally.

Before all of this you will need to be certain of a good supply of wood and somewhere to keep it. The longer wood is seasoned, the better it burns and the drier it is stored the better too (obviously!). If your fire has to evaporate water before it can burn the wood it will lose efficiency. You will also get more smoke, more complaints from the neighbours and dirty chimneys and bills and ruination!

Now this is probably illegal, and you didn't read it here, but the best place to get wood in the city is a walk in the park. Near us are a number of wooded parks and the council are forever felling trees and leaving the wood to rot. One large beech tree cut up over a fortnight will produce enough wood for a year's fires, and if you go for a walk when the men are doing their felling you can often get your wood for the price of a conversation.

The thing about burning wood in a wood burner is not to stoke it too high. Start your fire with newspaper and kindling and a log and then maybe put another smaller one on top while the first one is burning. This will then be enough for the night if you close the doors. There is really nothing extra to do, save backing the fire up for the night if you want to. A big log will burn slowly all night and still be alight in the morning. All you need to do is open the vent and it will burst into life once more.

Paper is another reasonable source of heat if you have enough. Simply shred it up and soak it in a little water to force it into briquette shapes. You can buy special moulds that expel most of the water, and you then leave them to dry. Mine have sometimes fallen apart as they burnt and have consequently been less efficient than wood, but they are always a good standby.

The thing to be sure of is that the wood is dry and of the right type, and although there are many reminders of which wood to burn on the internet, I prefer this one, which I think is a mix up of all the others and attributable to John Tams.

Wood - The Ideal Fuel

Logs to Burn, Logs to burn, Logs to burn,
Logs to save the coal a turn,
Here's a word to make you wise,
When you hear the woodman's cries.

Oak logs will warm you well,
If they're old and dry.
Larch logs of pine will smell,
But the sparks will fly.

Beech logs for Christmas time,
Yew logs heat well.
"Scotch" logs it is a crime,
For anyone to sell.

Birch logs will burn too fast,
Chestnut scarce at all.
Hawthorn logs are good to last,
If you cut them in the fall.

Holly logs will burn like wax,
You should burn them green,
Elm logs like smouldering flax,
No flame to be seen.

Pear logs and apple logs,
They will scent your room,
Cherry logs across the dogs,
Smell like flowers in bloom.

But ash logs, all smooth and grey,
Burn them green or old;
Buy up all that come your way,
They're worth their weight in gold.

The Urban Farmer

The Good Life Press
PO Box 536
Preston
PR2 9ZY
01772 652693

The Good Life Press Ltd. is a family run business specialising in publishing a wide range of titles for the smallholder, 'goodlifer' and farmer. We also publish **Home Farmer,** the monthly magazine for anyone who wants to grab a slice of the good life - whether they live in the country or the city.

Other Titles of interest

A Guide to Traditional Pig Keeping by Carol Harris
An Introduction to Keeping Sheep by J. Upton/D. Soden
Build It! by Joe Jacobs
Build It 2! by Joe Jacobs (due out 2009)
Build it...with pallets by Joe Jacobs (due out 2009)
The New Cottage Economy by Paul Peacock (due out 2009)
Craft Cider Making by Andrew Lea
First Buy a Field by Rosamund Young
Flowerpot Farming by Jayne Neville
Grow and Cook by Brian Tucker
How to Butcher Livestock and Game by Paul Peacock
Making Cordials and Meads by Marjorie Kimber (due out 2009)
Making Jams and Preserves by Diana Sutton
Making Sweets and sweetmeats by Marjorie Kimber (due out 2009)
Precycle! by Paul Peacock
Precycle 2! by Paul Peacock (due out 2009)
Preserving the Harvest by Diana Peacock (due out 2009)
Raising Chickens for Eggs and Meat by Mike Woolnough (due out 2009)
Talking Sheepdogs by Derek Scrimgeour
The Bread and Butter Book by Diana Sutton
The Cheese Making Book By Paul Peacock
The Pocket Guide to Wild Food by Paul Peacock
The Polytunnel Companion by Jayne Neville
The Sausage Book by Paul Peacock
The Secret Life of Cows by Rosamund Young
The Shepherd's Pup (DVD) with Derek Scrimgeour
Showing Sheep by Sue Kendrick
The Smoking and Curing Book by Paul Peacock
A Cut Above the Rest (A butchering DVD)

www.goodlifepress.co.uk
www.homefarmer.co.uk
www.precycle-it.co.uk